THROUGH THE GLASS

THE REALITY OF WORKING AT A FOR-PROFIT NEW YORK NURSING HOME DURING THE COVID-19 PANDEMIC

BY HELEN BEEDE

RoseDog Books

PITTSBURGH, PENNSYLVANIA 15238

RoseDog Books
585 Alpha Drive
Suite 103
Pittsburgh, PA 15238
Visit our website at www.rosedogbookstore.com

ISBN: 978-1-6376-4701-1
eISBN: 978-1-6376-4741-7

To my grandmother "Nanny" for listening to my stories every day after work, even when they are not interesting. And my adaptable grandfather "Papa" for taking on the household responsibilities so that she can live comfortably.

Table of Contents

CHAPTER 1: PURPOSE

Nursing homes are among the riskiest places to work and live during a pandemic. I wrote about my experience working in a nursing home in Upstate New York as COVID-19 continued to spread like wildfire throughout New York and the rest of the country. During this time, for-profit companies managing long-term care facilities were using the pandemic as an excuse to justify lobbying for monetary grants, less regulation, and protection against lawsuits from families with complaints related to COVID-19 deaths as well as more general allegations. As a result, they are closer to achieving the autonomy they have wanted all along. The for-profit nursing home industry is already notorious for a lack of accountability. This book reveals how the quality of care received by the residents in nursing homes is largely determined by how the businessmen running these facilities choose to interpret guidelines set forth by politicians.

We are living in unprecedented times in which there are still many unknowns. The healthcare industry has been challenged to great lengths and flooded with recommendations but doesn't always have the means to execute them. We have a responsibility to meet these challenges to the best of our ability with the resources at hand. Sometimes we have to settle for a plan B or C, which is acceptable. But when simple measures to reduce risk are ignored for others' comfort, greed, and/or reputation, this is a problem.

Nursing homes contain the most vulnerable people in our population. Most residents have chronic diseases which frequently require hospitalization, and others, like dialysis patients, require regular appointments out in the community to sustain life. Many have dementia and may not understand social distancing as they wander freely. Some of them are frightened to see staff walking around the building wearing masks.

The residents themselves are generally not masked because they are in their home. This means they are potentially exposing each other to illnesses they picked up during a recent hospitalization or appointment. Even when units are quarantined, each still contains over forty people in rooms off a narrow hallway. While the staff has it rough, the residents don't even get to leave the building every night and have not been able to see their families in person or attend group activities for months.

Not all privately operated nursing homes are run poorly. I have only worked for long-term care (LTC) facilities managed by corporations that handle several other buildings. It has given me the impression that the entire industry is corrupt. In speaking with others working in long-term care, some feel that single facilities run by one owner are generally a lot better. In these skilled nursing facilities, the conditions reflect more personally on that owner, and they want to take pride in their business. In contrast, corporations must support added layers of employees and it seems that nobody is held accountable for the quality of care. However, a 2019 assessment by the Long-Term Care Community Coalition concluded that the issue may be more about the conversion from non-profit or government-owned to for-profit than the fact that the for-profit is part of a chain. Between 2003-2017, for-profit nursing home ownership in New York grew from less than a 50 percent share in the market to over 60 percent.

I envy the facility pandemic responses at the workplaces of some of my friends in the field. A dietitian friend working at a smaller LTC facility nearby which is part of a for-profit chain was offered an additional five dollars per hour in hazard pay. She was expected to change into scrubs and put on a respirator and face shield upon entering the building. These precautions were taken even for her to walk through the building to her office, where she was encouraged to stay for the entirety of her shift. Another dietitian friend at a larger for-profit facility which is not part of a chain was instructed to stay home and quarantine for two weeks during an outbreak in her building. This friend tested negative but was still instructed to stay home for the full two weeks as a precaution because of mild respiratory symptoms.

Others, like the facility where I work, manage to go unnoticed by government regulators while blatantly ignoring public health recommendations. Out of the three nursing homes I've worked in, the one where I currently work is the best overall. It has a home-like atmosphere with more respectful interactions between and among residents and staff. The facility's weakest area, in my opinion, is infectious disease control. Unfortunately, this is a really bad time for this specific shortcoming.

Like many of the nursing homes making the news for COVID-19 deaths, this one has a record of deficiencies related to infectious disease control. I started my employment at this site in early March. Just two months prior, there had been over twenty deaths related to an influenza outbreak. This staggering death toll had led some staff to theorize that COVID-19 was actually the cause of death instead of influenza, but this was well before COVID-19 cases were confirmed in New York. I believe it was a very poorly controlled influenza outbreak. Regardless of the pathogen, you would think that having dealt with a disaster of this magnitude would have put this facility at an advantage for dealing with COVID-19. This was not the case by any means.

This facility is an example of why doing the right thing cannot be left to the discretion of individual businesses. There was no initiative taken on the part of the higher-ups in the building to put safeguards in place. Measures were only taken when their hands were forced by the governor's mandates or Department of Health requirements. And many of these measures were only followed when there was a perceived risk of being caught not following them.

The nursing home is run by a company which owns several others in the state. It is one of at least three chains in the area of which I am aware. There are also staffing agencies which provide much of the labor inside the buildings. These companies compete and also work together when it is mutually beneficial. These businesses are constantly evolving and growing. Working for a growing company means there is potential for employees to advance in their careers. This sounds promising for ambitious, career-focused individuals. But at what cost? These employees are forced to give up their integrity by going along with an administrator's wishes rather than following their own clinical judgment. If they do not, they know they will be forced out, often as a scapegoat for a deficiency exposed during a survey. So many employees learn to ignore certain realities for the sake of self-preservation.

The signs outside these facilities, like at many essential workplaces, announce "Heroes Work Here." But the staff inside are not treated like heroes. They have been deliberately kept in the dark about events going on in their own building. Their well-being and that of their families have been put at risk. And the responsibility is always put right back on them. With the lack of communication and ambiguity, it is easy to convince the staff that they are, in fact, the ones at fault.

Why am I qualified to tell this story? Considering how many articles have made the news about the horrors of long-term care facilities during this pandemic, there have been very few detailed stories explaining exactly how these types of events unfold. The staff inside the buildings experience the events firsthand. They have the best stories. But they are also exhausted. If they have not quit or been fired for speaking out, they are too burnt-out to come home and relive what they just went through. They want to try to forget about work as best they can so they can recharge a little before starting it all again the next day. Many have not even had the luxury of taking the full two-week quarantine break while sick with the virus.

Throughout this book, some of the staff are portrayed in a less than positive light in the described scenarios. I want to preface the story by saying that they are genuinely good people who care deeply for the residents. They are themselves the victims of a few forces at play. Mainly there is the pressure coming from corporate to put profit above all else. It is a business, after all. It is also obvious that some of them have not been taught the critical thinking skills to help them identify reliable sources of information. They accept the legitimate-enough sounding explanations they have been offered to justify unethical practices. They then pass these along to the staff below them. Accepting these explanations is easier and more comfortable than facing the truth. But the residents don't have a choice. And our comfort is not worth more than their lives.

The names of all staff and residents have been changed to respect their privacy. All racial, ethnic, religious, and other protected identifiers have also been omitted. This is unfortunate, because there are some amusing stories that could not be included for this reason. Facility names have also been fictionalized. All of the events, however, are real. Some of them can be shocking for people who have not worked in long-term care. This is an average nursing home. There are higher-quality nursing homes, and there are also worse ones. The COVID-19 outbreak here was pretty typical of what happened in other facilities. This is an insidious disease that has killed many nursing home residents.

We did not respond properly, however, and many of the illnesses and deaths could have been prevented. Residents were sent to the hospital and we would never hear about them again. I was disturbed when I realized I was losing track of residents and decided to start journaling for my own peace of mind. Many of my coworkers don't even realize the magnitude of the outbreak. I overheard one of the most reliable nurse managers telling a new staff member that we didn't have a lot of COVID-19 deaths. She was not lying. She was just unaware because she was not keeping a list compiled from many sources. Information was withheld, and it is easy to move on if we don't take a step back to process.

I have been piecing together this story after work and on weekends while working full-time at the nursing home. Each part has been written while I was in varying moods and at various stages of burnout. There was about a month when I completely stopped journaling. Committing to telling the story has given me a sense of purpose through times when I feel like I'm not having an impact. I have never written a book before, but I feel the story should be told from someone who is inside the nursing home daily. My purpose is not to create a literary masterpiece, but to hopefully bring some awareness to the seriousness of the situation in nursing homes. There is some medical jargon and acronyms, particularly when describing what was going on with residents during their illnesses. I have tried to minimize these terms or explain them as they come up to make the story more accessible to anyone interested in the situation at long-term care facilities, not just other medical professionals.

CHAPTER 2: SETTING THE SCENE

Of the many, many private LTC facilities of which I am aware of in the Upstate New York area, there are only two where I would feel safe as a patient. The waiting lists are longer for both, and one of them I could never afford. They are also the only facilities offering private rooms. Most places I have seen have rooms similar to those in a college dorm, where a small space is shared between two people. If you are standing in the doorway facing inward, there are two twin-sized beds along one side of the room with the heads of the beds against the wall. On the other side of the room is a window. There is often a dispute over which roommate is entitled to the window side. Each patient has a television along the wall across from their beds. The lighting is often dim, which necessitates the use of flashlights for detailed wound treatments and assessments. The atmosphere is also largely determined by the resident living inside the room. There are some residents with hoarding tendencies, and others who refuse to allow staff in for linen changes and cleaning. I enjoy going into the rooms of residents with artistic talent. Photographers and painters decorate the walls with their work.

There is no privacy, *ever,* and roommates are exposed to each other's illnesses. There is a curtain on a track on the ceiling which can be pulled around the bed for the illusion of privacy. I have been in facilities where these curtains are visibly dirty. They do not block out sound. Patients overhear each other's conversations with medical providers and family. Roommates are required to share a bathroom, and sometimes a bathroom is shared between adjoining rooms. There are also a few quads in many of these places. These rooms have a military barracks vibe with beds in all corners of the room. Somehow, the quads appeal to me more because they are a little more spacious and offer privacy due to the anonymity of being one amongst several.

The poorly run facilities oftentimes pay employees better than nicer ones because it is the only way to entice people to put up with the conditions. A bad facility can have very good employees. And they aren't usually drawn in just by the potentially higher pay. There is satisfaction in helping people who do not have the option to go somewhere nicer. Many have to work through the conflicting feelings of desiring to help these people and the need for self-preservation. Only a very small fraction of misdeeds ever become public knowledge. Most places will invest a lot more into public relations than in actually providing the services they advertise.

My grandmother had a stroke a few years before I went back to school to become a registered dietitian (RD). The first rehab center she went to was no good. During her short stay, she had to deal with several minor instances of poor customer service, like dinner one evening that consisted of two slices of white bread with a slice of Kraft Singles cheese. No veggie. No mayo. That was it. Other negative experiences were not so minor. One time she used her call light in the middle of the night for assistance getting to the bathroom. A young woman escorted her into the bathroom but didn't make it further than the mirror, where she couldn't resist stopping to primp and admire her own appearance. As she stroked her long hair, my grandmother tripped and almost fell. This caused the girl to swear and tell her that she would be using the bedpan from now on. My grandmother said that she didn't want to use the bedpan, and the girl told her that it wasn't up to her. My grandmother began to cry because she was not used to feeling so helpless or being treated like that, and the girl told her to stop being such a baby. All of these experiences made her question how she could have behaved differently to avoid them. Maybe if she had eaten better during the previous meal, she would not have offended the cook, and would have received a real dinner. Maybe if she had taken in less fluids throughout the day, she would not have been a nuisance to the night staff. She felt like she was being punished. And she is not high maintenance. Even if she were, these places are being paid to help people get through their most difficult times.

I was relieved when she moved to a nicer facility. I was working as a delivery driver during that time and would stop in to see her on my route, which took me into the area once or twice weekly. The food was fantastic and she adored the staff. She eats like a bird and would insist on sharing pieces of her meal. I did not know at the time that dietitians rely on intake data collected from meal trays, so her meal intakes looked a little better on the days I visited. She was alert, oriented, and happy in this facility, so I could be comfortable knowing that she was in good hands.

My first clinical job was at a place closer in quality to the first place my grandmother experienced. Arbor Park is a 200-bed facility in a low-income neighborhood and mainly serves its local residents. A friend had been excited about bringing me on because she knew I was not one of our diva classmates who might pull into the parking lot, see the place, and drive off. For the first several months of my employment, the dietitians were located in the education room. This was pretty sweet because it was spacious and had windows on a well-lit side of the building, so my spider plant "Vivvy" was thriving. There was a small bathroom by the room's entrance with the sink in the main area just next to the bathroom. Part of the furniture even included two hospital beds and dummies for the nursing aides to practice their skills on. This took some getting used to, especially when one would be moved. Usually the dummies would be lying in their beds, but occasionally you would walk in and one would be seated upright across the room.

There was a reason why I started the job based out of the education room. The actual diet office was in a shared suite with housekeeping on the other end of the ground floor. My position replaced a diet tech who I would meet in my next job a year later. Arbor Park was in an old building with leaks occurring on a regular basis. All offices were located on the first floor with the resident floors above and the kitchen in the basement. The two dietitians and diet tech had been moved out of their real office after a sudden flood of raw sewage burst down through the corner of the room. It rained down on the diet tech and ruined a laptop and a filing cabinet or two. This tech was a trooper, because she went home to shower and change and then returned to work to complete her day. I know if that had happened to me, it would have been the end of my workday. Even in the education room, there was a giant water-stained bubble growing in the ceiling by the entrance. One of our sticky notes on the corkboard recorded our bets for the exact date the bubble would burst.

Physical Therapy (PT) was located across from the education room. The PT director who was there when I first started was aggressive and self-absorbed. He would come into our office daily to use the restroom. He would spend up to twenty minutes at a time in there, so you knew he wasn't in there just taking a leak. When he would finally come out, he'd stroll by the sink just outside the door without stopping to wash his hands. I told the Speech and Language Pathologist (SLP) about this, and she shared why this was so disturbing—I mean, beyond the general nastiness of someone not washing their hands after pooping. Apparently after any contact at all with a resident, he would scrub his hands up to his elbows so thoroughly that it appeared he was about to perform a surgery. This could be triggered by something as simple as helping adjust someone who was slipping down in a wheelchair. This behavior showed that while he was concerned about germs *he* might pick up from a resident, he did not care about contaminating *them* with his feces.

The next incident I referred to as "the hot dog hissy fit." There was a woman with a developmental disability in one of the dining rooms who was having a full-on meltdown because she wanted a hot dog. And by meltdown, I mean there was furniture being flung around and it was quickly becoming hazardous to the staff and other residents. The administrator told the FSD (food service director) to go get a hot dog. He did not like being told what to do and became belligerent, yelling and refusing to comply. He ranted about this being the reason why "his" dietitians struggled to get certain residents' blood sugar under control. In actuality, he really did not care about our struggles or the patients unless there was an opportunity for conflict. He loved to be the macho man asserting himself. One of his supervisors was there during the incident and was trying to defuse the situation by volunteering to retrieve the hot dog. But the hot dog hissy fit ensued, and the administrator was pleased to have the opportunity to ask for the FSD's badge and kick him out of the facility. To be clear, my use of the phrase "hot dog hissy fit" refers to the behavior of the FSD, not the woman who was having a meltdown in the dining room.

We later found out that his aggressive tendencies were worse than we had realized. He once threatened to beat up one of his cooks in the parking lot. This cook was a tall, strongly built man with a military background. He had a calm, professional demeanor and was always dressed in a crisp, white chef's uniform. He was someone I would picture working in a five-star resort rather than at Arbor Park. He had responded to the FSD's invitation by saying something like, "Man, I could wreck you. Go settle down." The FSD's threats of violence weren't restricted to other men. The activities director at the time was a gorgeous, slender woman who was dating one of the kitchen supervisors. One time she tried to defend her boyfriend and the FSD threatened to "kick her ass."

Rather than being fired, he was placed in another facility. The regional director of nutrition services said that the new facility he was assigned to had some people with rough attitudes who could benefit from that type of personality. There was no communication about the situation to Arbor Park's kitchen employees who had been working under him. There was a man who was a floater with the staffing agency who would come in occasionally to put in food orders. There had been previous sexual harassment allegations against him and many felt uncomfortable having him in a position of power. For about a month, this lack of leadership and background drama got in the way of patient care.

It was at Arbor Park that I first learned of the sketchy infectious disease practices in long-term care facilities. They are not hospitals. They are skilled medical facilities, but they are also homes. For this reason, it is difficult to balance the need to protect the staff and residents from each other's pathogens with preserving the dignity of the residents. Facilities can receive tags from the state survey crews related to either. In a hospital, you would not see somebody with infectious diarrhea or an antibiotic-resistant pathogen wandering about. This is commonplace in LTC.

In one instance, I was concerned about a woman with clostridium difficile, or what we call C. diff, who kept coming downstairs to visit the administrative staff and vending machines. Visiting is a normal occurrence under healthy circumstances. C. diff is a highly infectious bacterium that causes watery diarrhea which has a strong, distinctive odor. It most commonly occurs in people who are constantly on broad-spectrum antibiotics. These kill off the beneficial bacteria in the colon, which assist in keeping harmful bacteria from proliferating. I voiced my concern regarding this woman coming downstairs, to which I received a sharp reply from the infectious disease nurse about it being the patient's right to have freedom of movement around the building and that her C. diff was basically resolved. A few days later, I saw the same woman strolling down the hallway with her walker, headed toward the vending machines. She was wearing shorts with an obvious spot of liquid feces on the back. This was brought to the attention of nursing, and they finally did something about it.

Another common element in the industry is employees tend to bounce around LTC facilities, so it's best not to burn any bridges. I ultimately ended up covering the Arbor Park 200-bed facility as the lone dietitian for an extended period of time—working ten-plus hour days with promises of overtime pay or time off which never panned out. That was the last straw, so I took a job with another outsourced company that specialized in positions for clinical RDs. I made $10,000 more per year and was able to focus exclusively on my clinical work because the food service department was separate. At

Arbor Park, the lazy FSDs required the dietitians to print all meal tickets, production sheets, menus, and snack labels, even though there were four supervisors in the kitchen. These secretarial tasks took precedence, which left little time to focus on our high-risk residents. Having a diet tech at the new job also saved me a lot of time because she took care of customer service tasks and most communication with the kitchen. This allowed me time to refine my clinical practice.

There are always trade-offs. Falls View was about a forty-minute drive from home and did not have the friendly coworker vibe of Arbor Park. At Falls View, in contrast, the nursing department maintained its hostility toward other departments. I worked for a better company, but the facility was rough due to the general culture of a disrespectful staff. It was difficult to get the job done when tracking down a nursing aide or kitchen worker was necessary. Staff in these lower-paid positions would wander off frequently when needed or roll their eyes and give excuses for not being able to assist. The building itself was beautiful and spacious, with a newer feel. If managed appropriately, it could easily be a five-star facility. Part of the challenge stemmed from its size and location. It is a very large facility in a country location and could hold more residents than Arbor Park. It also had an adult daycare. However, it was difficult to maintain enough staff to keep the place running. If someone showed up to work regularly and could complete their job, a bad attitude was overlooked.

At Falls View, there was one licensed practical nurse (LPN) we referred to as the "sausage queen" because she would frequently request extra sausage and other energy-dense snacks with little nutritional value for her residents. She would do this regardless of therapeutic diet recommendations. There was one gentleman struggling with fluid accumulation whom she insisted on serving extra sausage daily despite the harm of high sodium for a person with this type of condition. This man's overall experience in the facility was very degrading, and when he left, he was basically on his deathbed. I was pleasantly surprised to find out via a social media page that he was well and thriving after getting out of there. This social media page was not the most reliable source of information, but I have gained updates on a couple former residents from it. The page is run by someone in the rural county where Falls View is located. It contains stories about local scandals, usually of a political nature.

Let us briefly visit the topic of the LPN positions. To become an LPN, a nurse must complete a twelve-month vocational program. The registered nurse (RN), on the other hand, must complete a minimum of a two-year degree. It is common in long-term care facilities for LPNs to hold unit manager positions, which are the leadership roles serving as liaisons between upper-level management and those working the floor. The registered nurse (RN) credential is preferred for these roles, but there is never a waiting list of RNs interested in working in these facilities, so the LPN holds the position for long periods of time. There are several tasks which only an RN is qualified to perform. Some examples include fall assessments, care plan reviews and running IV lines. When an LPN is running a unit, RNs from another unit or someone from one of the administrative nursing positions are pulled in as needed to complete the RN tasks.

There are some frustrations created by this dynamic. Oftentimes an LPN given one of the management positions develops a sense of entitlement. I have seen over and over again the situation where a facility will hire a new RN and the LPN gets offended when it's time to step down to a charge nurse position and relinquish the unit manager role. Charge nurse positions are still management positions, but they usually entail more hands-on work such as running a med cart. To some extent, I understand their frustration, because oftentimes the RNs coming on board are lazy and/or incompetent nurses who have been able to coast along in this practice area because of their more advanced credentials. And the transition is often less than respectful. I have seen LPNs learn that they're being replaced in a morning report when the new RN unit manager is introduced on their first day. One time I was standing behind a new unit manager while waiting in line for COVID-19 testing. I watched the awkward introduction as she met the LPN she was replacing for the first time. It was the woman performing her COVID-19 test.

This just about catches us up to pandemic time. My coworker noticed an online ad for the RD position in a facility in my town. Dutch Meadows is run by the same company as Falls View and is serviced by the same outsourced RD company that I was working for, so the transition was simple. It felt like getting a raise to move to a smaller, more pleasant facility within a six-minute drive from my apartment. The facility could accommodate about 130 residents over three units. The single-story building has the administrative offices in the center with the units fanning out in a cloverleaf shape. One unit is the dedicated rehab unit, with the other two housing more long-term residents. In general, it has a much homier vibe compared to the institution-like feel of Falls View. I didn't have much time to settle in before we started to feel the first effects of the pandemic.

Chapter 3: The Preparations

The first restriction placed on long-term care facilities at the onset of the COVID-19 pandemic was the rule prohibiting non-medically necessary visits after March 13, 2020, at five p.m. These places are homes to the most medically vulnerable population and could not risk someone's asymptomatic grandchild introducing the virus. Both residents and staff seemed to understand the reasoning behind the rule, but that didn't mean there wasn't a high level of disappointment. When these mandates are put in place, they are typically effective immediately.

One woman's daughter had flown in from Florida the day before and had planned to spend a lot of time with her mother over the next several days. She was able to come once before the mandate. I believe the facility did slightly bend the rules in light of this extenuating circumstance by allowing the family to come the next day for a visit in the conference room, which was then disinfected. The rules were also bent for people who had family members who were actively dying. However, family could not come in if the reason for their loved one's passing was COVID-19. There was also a time when no family was allowed in the building regardless of the family member's reason for passing.

Shortly after the rule went into effect, you would see the heartwarming stories on the news about window visits at nursing homes around the state. The family member would call on their cell phone from outside the closed window, or if the resident was on a second floor or above, they could open the window and speak normally. At Dutch Meadows, these unscheduled visits were tolerated at first. Then a visitor was caught standing outside of one of the rooms and speaking through the open ground floor window. The receptionist on that unit was livid because she cared for her elderly mother at home and was terrified of bringing the virus home to her. This incident occurred in the rehab unit, which was the worst place to have a breach in protocol because another way in which the facility prepped for the pandemic was by containing the higher risk patients in that one unit. These high-risk patients consisted of dialysis patients and new admissions.

Dialysis patients went out into the community three times per week for their appointments. New admissions usually came in from the hospital, where they could have been exposed. They were monitored closely for two weeks before being moved onto another unit. Other concerns about the window visits involved the invasion of privacy of the other residents as people walked around looking for the correct room. The facility also did not want to get sued if someone tripped while tromping around in the bushes. Therefore, the window visits were temporarily halted until the activities staff was assigned the task of scheduling them in a more controlled way.

Since group activities were banned around the same time and we were no longer allowed to have visitors, the activities staff organized all forms of alternative visits—most of them were through Zoom. The main dining room was just outside of my office, and it was officially closed. Prior to the pandemic, the majority of group activities were also held in this room. From bingo games to crafting to pet therapy, there was usually a lively scene nearby and it was a great way to get to know the residents on a more personal level. The Elvis impersonator was one of the most well-attended events.

Staff were required to wear surgical masks at all times and get their temperature taken when reporting for their shift. There were some issues to work through with both of these new rules. It was not clear at first where to find the thermometer. It was in the nursing supervisor's office 40 percent of the time, in the infectious disease nurse's office 40 percent of the time, at the front desk 10 percent of the time, and completely missing on one of the units 10 percent of the time. We used one of the thermometers that go in the ear with single-use disposable covers. Sometimes we would run out of these. Sometimes there was nobody actually available to take the temperatures, so it was an honor system to write down your own temp in the logbook. This eventually became a smoother process when the facility acquired a contactless thermometer and the task was officially the responsibility of whoever was manning the front desk.

There was also the frustrating situation of a lack of any type of protocol for people who spiked a fever. I shared an office with two other women: Meg, the MDS (minimal data set) coordinator, and Amanda, the activities director. Amanda is a young woman who struggles with a painful medical condition which requires medication that dulls her immune system. One morning, her temperature was taken twice with varying degrees of fever each time. Rather than send her home, she was instructed to continue working while "isolating" in our office with plans to take her temperature again in the afternoon. The well-being of the other two staff in that office was never questioned. Our desks are situated on one side of the office facing opposite walls. When we are both working in the office at the same time, the backs of our chairs are nearly touching, and we have to be mindful not to bump into each other. I considered her to be like my canary in a coal mine because of her immune-compromised status. I figured that once she started showing symptoms, it was time to get worried. Meg is probably about six feet from our desks, which is good because she exercises more caution than anyone else in the place.

At some point, there was a rule set that we could not leave the facility during our workday. I wasn't really sure if this was just a facility rule or if it was their interpretation of a state mandate. It seemed a little arbitrary considering that our movement was unrestricted before and after work. We could order delivery food, but we could not go out to pick something up ourselves. We had a lot of food gifted to us during this time anyway. Supportive family members would send doughnuts, pizza, subs, and breakfast sandwiches. It would have been a difficult time for anyone on a diet. I continued my lunch break walks during this time.

Nobody gave me a hard time about it, and I figured it was okay because I was not entering any businesses. I don't remember this rule ever officially being lifted. It just seemed like people got sick of it after a while and started going back out.

The administrator, Chad, announced that the facility had the green light to go by a different set of rules than those suggested by the Centers for Disease Control (CDC) and Department of Health (DOH). Most people were required to quarantine for two weeks if they had a COVID-19 diagnosis. Healthcare workers in any setting were only required to quarantine for one week because these workers were so in demand. At our facility, if we became short-staffed, we were expected to defer to the facility for guidance. For staff members who were sick but not on their deathbeds, this meant not even quarantining for the full week. Later on, the two-week quarantine requirement extended to healthcare workers as well.

I considered morning report to be the riskiest part of the entire day. This is a meeting that takes place in every long-term care facility. It's usually at nine a.m. and begins with the department heads sharing any important information. Then everyone is excused except for the clinical team. The unit managers each review their units, and then we discuss falls and room changes. This meeting theoretically could be over within half an hour, but that is never the case. It usually takes about an hour but can extend to two hours on a rough day. Things can get pretty emotional too.

This meeting is held in the conference room, where as many people as can fit crowd around the table in the center of the room. Some of the non-clinical staff stand around the edges because they are excused when the clinical portion of the meeting begins. Those at the table—the administrator, director of nursing (DON), assistant director of nursing (ADON), who also serves the infectious disease and staff education roles, social worker(s), unit managers, therapy director, dietitian, and admissions director— are packed in within one foot of each other. One of the things that bothered me most about the facility's handling of the situation was that basic social distancing protocols were never encouraged in this daily meeting. We were hypocritically instructed to remind staff at the nursing stations to not congregate, while we sat around a crowded table every morning without masks. We were not told that we could not wear our masks. But with the administrator, DON, and ADON not setting this precedent, it would have put the staff under them in an awkward position to protest by wearing our masks.

Literally nothing changed with regards to that procedure at any point during the outbreak in our facility. I'm writing this after the illness has already ripped through the place. I understand that risk cannot be completely eliminated from these workplaces. But there are several ways in which the morning report procedure could have been changed in order to protect the staff required to report for it. These changes would be simple and cost nothing, but comfort is repeatedly chosen over doing the right thing. People could (a) be required to wear their mask or, better yet, (b) move the meeting to the much larger and currently unused dining room.

When COVID-19 first came to our region, the common areas in the building were cleaned more frequently. There were housekeepers washing down the walls throughout the building. This seemed to be happening regularly. This may have continued after our first several cases, but it did not last long. One potential source of contamination that has always sketched me out in the building is the bathroom situation. There are two single-stall bathrooms for all of the staff. In order to use one of these, you must grab a key from the front desk. I am not sure if the keys are ever disinfected. If they are, it is not very often. Sometimes you will grab one and realize that it's wet. It's something that you try not to think about. But you do. There is a hook on the inside of each bathroom door, so it seems like a no-brainer that you should hang the key on the door hook and not grab it again until you have washed your hands and are ready to leave.

The fact that the keys are sometimes speckled with water means that some staff members put the key on the sink. So, it could be getting the splash back from their hands when they're washing up. There has been some research suggesting a possible gastrointestinal (GI) route of COVID-19 transmission. Not that the virus itself matters in this case. I would prefer not to be exposed to someone's norovirus either. The walls are not cleaned in the bathroom. Ever. There have been boogers stuck to the wall, specifically in one of the bathrooms which I first noticed months ago. Either a staff member regularly uses this wall for booger flicking, or they have been collecting over a long period of time from people sneezing while on the toilet.

Since other countries, New York City, and Washington state had already been affected by COVID-19, we had the advantage of being aware of potential worst-case scenarios from shocking news stories. There were reports of nursing homes with bodies piling up and staff panicking and abandoning their residents. The most morbid discussion we had to have was planning the makeshift morgue. This would be the space where bodies would have to be stored in the event that deaths occurred in the area at such a rapid rate that funeral homes were unable to keep up. The dayroom in the rehab unit was chosen for this purpose. The plan was to crank up the air-conditioning in the room to slow decomposition.

We had to plan for severe staffing shortages, which could happen due to several reasons. Multiple staff could be out sick with the virus, since direct care staff are at very high risk. The other possibility was that people may panic and bail on their jobs. Whatever the cause, it was important to make sure that the residents were not abandoned. The plan was for staff from other departments to take a daylong crash course and then be turned loose to provide care. We were even encouraged to invite people we knew but who were not employees who may be interested in helping out. To my knowledge, we never did get any community helpers. This was allowed during the crisis, and once staffing levels returned to normal, these staff members would no longer be considered qualified to provide care. Feeding was the one task that was not covered under this plan. This required separate certification, and some staff members at Falls View took this course in preparation. The crash course enabled staff to help with tasks such as toileting, hygiene, turning and positioning, and dressing.

All staff positions in nursing homes were considered essential. Some of the positions, however, could have been done remotely at least some of the time. We were required to fulfill all of our hours in person. I wondered if the reasoning was related to planned staffing shortages and the potential for those staff to have to slide into direct care roles. Secretarial roles, admissions, and billing are a few of the jobs that did not seem to require full-time in-person staffing. I could do the majority of my job remotely. More likely, everyone's presence was required to keep things running as smoothly and as normally as possible for the emotional well-being of the remaining staff and residents.

Being an outsourced employee, I wasn't sure what would be expected of me if we got to the point where non-clinical staff started filling direct care roles. Since my pay came from the outsourced company, I wondered if I would have to get on the facility's payroll to cover my overtime. I reached out to my regional supervisor. The bulk of my company's employees work in the New York City/New Jersey region, but somehow none of the facilities had reached this crisis level. She made the recommendation to first offer my services to other departments such as the kitchen or front desk. I had already considered the possibility of helping Sue, our overworked social worker. My undergraduate degree is in psychology, and I'm pretty good at de-escalating, so it could theoretically work.

When I started the job, there was a second social worker who had just started a week or two before me. During discussions about the virus, there were people who talked about the potential for bailing once it got into the building. He was one among several. He appeared to be a fairly healthy man in his twenties, but he felt that he was immune-compromised and at risk due to having Lyme disease. He was the only staff member that I knew of who followed through and left the job when the virus hit. He did not wait for it to break out. Once we had our first confirmed case in the hospital, he wasn't messing around, and he left. He changed his story around his reason for leaving, though. When he finally did leave, he said it was because he lived with his parents and wanted to protect them. That does sound more diplomatic than bailing for your own protection. Whichever the reason, it was smart for him to leave if he was unwilling to risk contracting the virus himself or bringing it into his household. Workers in healthcare settings are always at risk. And this place did little to protect their residents and employees.

For several weeks, starting March 25th, nursing homes in New York were required to take back their residents who tested positive for COVID-19 in the hospital. They were also forced to take new admissions who had tested positive for the virus if they were medically stable and would otherwise be accepted if it were not for their COVID-19 status. There was also a restriction on testing these residents to make sure that they were not still infected. The purpose of this mandate was to remove some of the burden from the hospitals in hopes that more lives would be saved by opening up beds in hospitals than would be lost from introducing the virus into nursing homes.

This was the one rule I was 100 percent okay with the facility sleazing its way around. Technically, you did not need to accept these patients if you could not safely accommodate them. I know that the facility would not have admitted to being unable to accommodate patients, even if that had been the case, because then we would miss out on profits. I think they just came up with reasons other than facility inadequacy in order to turn away these potential residents. One such method was saying that we didn't have rooms available to accommodate the gender of the person in question.

CHAPTER 4: COVID-19 ARRIVES AND SPREADS UNCHECKED

After our first several cases, it was becoming stressful seeing patients go out to the hospital and never hearing about them again. I started journaling daily to help keep track of these people for my own sanity. I would put a box around the names of people who were officially diagnosed with the illness. If they passed, I would put a single line through their name with the date of their passing, if known. For those who were in the hospital, the admissions ladies were the best source of information. I'm not sure how much information they were officially allowed to receive. There are probably rules that enable them to get updates on those residents with a bed hold in the facility, but not others. They had regular contact with the hospitals and could usually get updates regardless. Each of the cases described in this story has a corresponding number in parentheses. The numbers show the order in which I found out about the case and recorded it in my journal. I pulled information from many different sources, so some cases were confirmed months after they occurred. Since the story follows the timeline, and the cases and information were obtained at different times, the corresponding case numbers are not always in chronological order.

The first case occurred in a well-loved resident (1) who was a dialysis patient undergoing cancer treatment. Despite his extreme physical discomfort, he always remained pleasant. He was sociable and spent a lot of time in the common areas, and staff members were always giving him hugs. He spiked a fever on April 2nd and was not supposed to be sent out for his dialysis treatment that morning. Somehow this message was not properly communicated, and he was sent out anyway. The dialysis clinic was very upset and sent him to the hospital to be tested. Our facility received a tag for this incident. He tested positive in the hospital and passed after a short battle with the illness. Many people were deeply affected by losing this man, not just because it was our first case, but also because he was a wonderful person. A memorial was held just outside the building. I heard the singing through the open conference room window. A unit manager brought up the sad truth that we would most likely have too many deaths in the near future to pay respects to everyone in this way.

This gentlemen's roommate was tested for the virus. He was the first resident tested in the facility. Luckily, he tested negative. The test for COVID-19 is a nasopharyngeal swab. It is very invasive, uncomfortable, and not completely without risk. This man developed a severe nosebleed the next day. I remember this day clearly because we were in the middle of care conferences. Every resident has care conferences shortly after admission and then every three months afterward. It is a time for all disciplines to come together with the resident and their family to discuss their progress. This man's nosebleed was serious enough that nurses were pulled out of the meetings to handle the situation. These risks are actually pretty rare, but this incident greatly contributed to my initial fear of the test.

The second case (2) occurred shortly afterward. This was a man in his mid-sixties who had been experiencing a declining appetite since February. At first, he was still taking in fluids, but by his last week in the facility, he was receiving clysis. This rehydration technique is considered old school but is making a comeback in a lot of long-term care facilities. In this procedure, fluids are given subcutaneously. It's simple and more cost-effective than IV fluids and is often used when finding a vein becomes difficult. Most residents have regular lab work every three months. He had some concerning results on April 8th which indicated kidney failure. He was sent out to the hospital on this day, when he tested positive for the virus and also died.

There was a third man (3) who was sent out and tested positive in the hospital. He had a couple of documented falls the first week in April as well as a poor appetite. He first spiked a fever on April 13th and was sent to the hospital upon the family's request on the 15th. I always wondered what happened to him and only learned his fate several months later when I asked the admissions director. He had expired in the hospital. And by expired, I mean died. I'm only using the term this one time in order to remark on its use in long-term care facilities. When the death of a resident is discussed among coworkers, the resident is said to have expired.

There are differing opinions on the use of this word. Some feel it's less blunt than the word "dead." Others, including myself, find the word to be offensive. It just makes me think of rotten food being tossed out of a refrigerator. I don't believe that any of the nurses would use this word when informing a family member about their loved one's passing.

I didn't find out until over a month later that a man in his mid-seventies (32) had spiked a fever a couple of days before our first known case was discovered in the dialysis patient. He was put on antibiotics. There was no coughing or shortness of breath (SOB) noted. A chest X-ray showed no signs of acute illness. Almost two weeks later, his appetite decreased. He spiked a fever again and had diminished respiratory effort. He was not responding to verbal stimuli. He was arousable, but lethargic. His family was contacted and his wife was in agreement that comfort measures were best. He had advanced dementia and was not able to communicate how he was feeling throughout the illness. He was given supplemental oxygen and his O2 saturation improved from 73 percent to 90 percent. He lost his ability to swallow.

He passed away the next day. His wife was at his bedside. At this time, there was an exception to the no visitor rule if the resident was actively dying. This rule only applied to those residents who did not have COVID-19. Eventually, no family was allowed in the building regardless of their loved one's reason for dying. She would not have been able to be there for his passing if he had received a positive COVID-19 test. His is a confusing case because I was later told by admissions that he was COVID-19 positive. It is possible that a test was obtained and we didn't receive the results until after his death.

The choices made by the leadership over the following two weeks were inexcusable and allowed the virus to infiltrate the entire facility. Chad had mentioned during preparation discussions at morning report that he expected the virus would reach us eventually, but that for public relations reasons, we absolutely could not be one of the first five facilities in the area to be hit. There were several individuals who were symptomatic in the facility during this time. They were not restricted in their movement around the building. They were not tested for the virus. A resident unexpectedly passed away. He was noted to be SOB the day before.

During this period, the fevers were explained away by urinary tract infections (UTIs). UTIs are a somewhat common occurrence in a nursing home, but it got ridiculous. There was a man who spiked fevers off and on during this entire period. They retrieved a urine sample and somehow it didn't make it to the lab for analysis. When this was discovered, it was never clear if they ever tried to get another sample. It seemed more likely it was just ignored. The man then developed respiratory symptoms. He began to cough badly and was producing a lot of mucous. The DON, Karen, physically assisted him to clear mucous to help him breathe easier. She was not wearing personal protective equipment (PPE) other than the surgical mask required while in the building.

The infectious disease nurse had ordered the dining room closed at the start of the restrictions, but Chad was constantly undermining this decision. There were a handful of residents who would wander in there and hang out. This very sick man was one of them. One afternoon as I finished my work for the last couple hours of my day, I was horrified as I continuously heard his wet cough. When I finally left for the day, he was posted by the dining room exit. I had to step around the wheelchair within two feet to get out. He had a trash can next to him and a roll of paper towels on his lap to deal with the amount of mucous he was producing. There were at least two activities aides seated at a table in the corner of the room within six feet.

Although he was so sick, there was no effort made to keep him in his room or even on the unit. One day he saw some coroners wheeling a body down the hallway and had a meltdown. Sue felt terrible and brought this up in morning report. She thought that something should be done so that residents did not see their neighbors being carted away. None of the decision-makers seemed to pay much attention to this opinion.

On Monday, April 20th, we learned that there were five positive cases and seventeen others being monitored for fever in the building. These people were being followed on line lists, which are a way to track outbreak information. Somebody had apparently forced some testing or it was deemed acceptable because enough other local LTC facilities had been in the news with cases. One of the positives was the man just discussed (5). He passed away the next day. Amanda took his passing hard. He was a nuisance at times, bothering the female residents, but he seemed to take to Amanda. He was her favorite. Amanda was the only activities staff member allowed to work with confirmed positive cases. She enabled him to speak with his family through video chat for the last time on Monday afternoon. He died just before morning report on Tuesday.

Once we had confirmed positive cases in the building, we were instructed to keep this information from the direct care staff. We were told that the reason for this was to avoid panic and staff walkouts. Staff were only told on a "need to know" basis. It was not okay, because multiple people enter rooms on a daily basis: housekeepers, therapists, etc. The word HIPAA—which stands for the Health Insurance Portability and Accountability Act which is designed, in part, to protect patients' privacy—was thrown around to keep people from talking out of fear of breaking patient privacy laws. But it really wasn't applicable. The staff were not even to know that we had COVID-19 in the building.

This is not to say that walkouts were not a concern. A nurse friend in a corporate position at one of the other big long-term care companies was working at a facility on the other side of the state. Aides and nurses working on the two units, which had COVID-19 positive residents, just bailed. Nurses had left the keys on their med carts and walked out, so my friend was mandated to work the floor. This place was providing good PPE too. She sent over a selfie looking pretty hardcore with a face shield, which was required just to walk the hallways. She could not believe that the staff would just abandon their residents. She had told me about the staff in this place prior to the outbreak, however. She said they made Falls View look like a five-star facility. I replied, "So it's similar to Arbor Park?" She had also worked in both of these facilities. She replied, "This place makes Arbor Park look like all their staff took etiquette classes on the weekends."

Therefore, the reasoning behind keeping these people in the dark made sense for the facility. The lack of PPE may have even assisted in keeping everyone calm. Maybe the face shields in the facility across the state were too much of a visual reminder that this was getting real. But these people would find out sooner or later, and it would have been better to let them know right away. I believed that this decision was made, in part, to avoid visiting the hazard pay topic. They probably did not want to admit that they did not have enough PPE to protect everyone who would be coming in contact with these people. This was not entirely the facility's fault. There was a national shortage. But they should have been straightforward about it. The staff were not given the choice to make informed decisions about their own health and that of their families.

They would go through varying degrees of secrecy. Sometimes the positive diagnoses were common staff knowledge. Other times it was only the specific staff working with those residents who were in the know. This made the PPE situation precarious because staff were turned away when requesting N95 respirators if they were not working with a confirmed positive patient. On the other hand, we were told to assume everyone was positive. Assuming everyone was positive was the smartest way to work because it was well known that the majority of cases were asymptomatic. And we weren't testing many people at all—symptomatic or not.

A man in his early seventies (4) spiked a fever on April 13th, almost exactly a month after his admission to the facility. The next day he complained of feeling sick to his stomach. He had nausea and vomiting that resolved after a day. He had an unwitnessed fall in the bathroom a few days later. A COVID-19 test was completed the next day and the positive results came back quickly. His fever was intermittent throughout his two-week illness. There were a few mentions of mild respiratory symptoms. He was started on morphine for comfort and passed away a few days later.

The roommate of this man became very ill but was never tested. He was one of my favorites at the time and had not been at the facility long. He had a very involved niece who was concerned about his meal intakes. Conversation came easily with this man. He told me that he had not been ill since the age of seventeen—no colds, nothing. And he was a bus driver, so I'm sure there was plenty of exposure. He was not depressed but was ready to pass on. His wife and only child, a daughter, had already passed away. The illness took him. Since he was never tested, he was never included in the count. But his roommate died from the illness (4). So most likely, it was COVID-19.

Three of the five residents who were announced positive in the first group have since passed. The third was a woman who was in her early nineties (8). She had fevers for several weeks but seemed to be recovering very well. I would occasionally catch headlines about centenarians recovering from the illness and was excited that she was going to pull through. She abruptly took a turn for the worse and passed away on April 28th. I have seen this happen a few times. A few residents seemed to have a false recovery period and then quickly decline and pass away. Some of the cases which presented in this way may have been attributed to cytokine storms during which the body begins to attack its own cells. These intense immune responses have occurred in severely ill COVID-19 patients.

There was one man in the group who recovered and went home (7). He hadn't been in the facility for very long and may have even come in from the hospital with the illness. The facility had reservations about accepting this guy because we had his father the month prior; the man was an absolute nightmare, and was constantly threatening violence on people. He threatened to break the male social worker's legs at one point. So, there was concern that the new guy would be like his father. He knew that his father had been in the facility and assured the staff that he hated his father and had not seen him in decades. For a few days, he had us fooled.

But his father's genes ran strong, and it wasn't long before he became aggressive. After his diagnosis, he wandered around the facility and announced that he wanted to spread the illness around. This situation was discussed in morning report with the decision to call the cops if he did that again. He was scheduled for a care conference the next day. Sue and I decided that it would be safest to have his meeting as a teleconference since residents have phones in their rooms. Chad told us that at least one person had to be there in person because we could not treat this man like a leper. Given that Chad had shown zero regard for the safety of his staff in any other instance, we chose to ignore this demand. We called him up for his meeting. It was not productive; he was angry with the facility because his blood sugars were high and his requests for extra food were not fully satisfied. I offered nutrition education, which he declined. He would only be satisfied if I granted his request for several sandwiches in addition to the regular entrée with each meal and somehow made this not affect his blood sugar. I had no regrets about not visiting this man in person.

The last member of the group was a woman whom I had seen for a care conference and wound rounds the week beforehand (6). She was still hanging on, but not thriving. She was down to seventy-six pounds despite dietary interventions. She was very fatigued when working with therapy. The doctor prescribed Marinol to try to increase her appetite. The purpose of her admission to the facility was to gain weight and strength before restarting cancer treatment. She had since been in and out of the hospital and there had been talk of comfort care measures. For almost six months there was no change in her status and I did not think she would survive. Then in October, she triggered for a significant weight gain. I assumed it was an erroneous weight and requested a reweight. I met with her and she was thriving and had strong motivation to continue making progress to return home to her boyfriend and cat. She also told me that the cancer diagnosis had been in error. I had to fight back tears of relief and happiness while taking in this unexpected positive development.

The handling of the situation after these initial five residents were diagnosed in-house continued to defy logic. It seemed like you could not be more efficient in setting up an environment to contaminate the entire facility. Two of the positives were housed in separate quads. Two of my dialysis residents were rooming with positives. There was no communication about how they would decide who to test. We were told that there would be some testing on asymptomatic people because the DOH was requiring it.

CHAPTER 5: MY COVID-19 INFECTION

Around this time, I started to suspect that I might be carrying the virus. On a Thursday afternoon, I began to experience some bizarre changes in taste. At this point, the loss of taste/smell was not one of the better-known symptoms. We were watching out for fevers, cough, and shortness of breath. The loss of taste was more noticeable than the loss of smell; however, there were a couple of instances where I realized my sense of smell was not there either. When I was riding by a farm with my husband, Mark, over the weekend, he commented that it smelled really bad. I grew up in Vermont and am very familiar with the strong odor of fertilizer from dairy farms. I can even detect the difference between natural and synthetic fertilizers. I smelled nothing. I also noticed at some point that there was a banana peel in the trash can by my desk at work and I hadn't taken it out for a few days. This realization made me slightly self-conscious that the smell could have been noticeable to my office mates and I was doing nothing about it.

I started doing a little research and decided that I should inform the infectious disease nurse when I came in on Monday. She mentioned that there had been some recent articles suggesting that loss of taste/smell may be a symptom. I was looking for a little direction—like did she want me to get tested? I mentioned my intention to call the hotline to schedule a test. She did not offer an opinion on whether or not I should get tested or be in the building, but she did say that if I chose to get tested, I would have to be out following the test until the results were processed. I did not see this as a problem as I felt the majority of my tasks could be completed remotely. I had even been emailing myself regularly with updated documents that were on my work desktop just in case I needed to quarantine.

The previous two weeks had shown that my facility was taking the "no news is good news" approach by not testing or isolating even the symptomatic residents. I mentioned that I would keep my mask on during morning report. I was very annoyed by her response, which was: "Well, you should be wearing your mask anyway." This lady literally sat next to me in morning report most days and, like everyone else, her mask was off the entire time. NOBODY wore a mask at that table. Our FSD was the only one who wore a mask during the meeting, while he stood at the edge of the room. He had poorly controlled diabetes and felt he should take precautions. Unfortunately, the best way for him to be safe would have been for everyone else to wear a mask as well. They are designed to contain the wearer's germs and protect others more than provide self-protection. This is the perfect example of the ambiguity around what we were supposed to be doing and putting the blame back on staff who did not subscribe to the shared delusion that we were and always had been following the rules all along.

I also felt that I would be judged for being paranoid or high maintenance. But I had been judging my coworkers who continued to show up to work symptomatic and did not want to do the same. There was the unspoken message that I could do nothing and continue to work. I reached out to my outsourced company via email for more definitive guidance and to voice my concerns regarding the facility's poor COVID-19 response and was met with more ambiguity. The vice president said she was glad that I wasn't experiencing fever, SOB, or cough. She connected me with the human resource (HR) lady, who responded five days later with the advice to call my healthcare clinic if I continued to experience fever, cough, or SOB (which I had clearly communicated I had not). Even if I had, there were no timeline recommendations. Her email stated that my physician would determine if I needed to be actively tested for COVID-19. If I received a positive result, I was to send the documentation. The message ended with a link to a CDC webpage.

The VP and regional supervisor stressed that they were working in conjunction with the facilities and that all facilities were responding differently. There was no acknowledgement of the details I gave regarding how poor the response was in my facility other than a "thank you for sharing all of this information." Prior to me reaching out, the only correspondence I'd received from my company regarding COVID-19 had been a letter of access indicating that I was an essential employee at the end of March and an email on April 1st with links to CDC pages. It would not be until July 23rd that an email was sent out reviewing the proper use of

PPE. It would eventually become clear that the company's main focus was to please their customers, not to protect their staff.

I decided to do the right thing and go get tested. The Department of Health had a hotline that you could call for screening. I called that day and was scheduled for the following day at one thirty. I was afraid of the test itself because I had seen it performed on my husband a month prior. He received a throat culture, which I absolutely hate, and said that was actually the easy part. A nasopharyngeal swab was performed on him too; it was quick and looked a bit rough. A long rod was just jammed up in there and pulled back out immediately. He compared it to checking the oil in a car. He was uncomfortable for at least half an hour after the test. He was also vague in describing his discomfort because he didn't want to scare me, knowing that I'd probably need to get this done eventually. It would have been better if he had just come right out and said it was the worst thing ever.

There were social fears related to the test results as well. Mark was tested right after his office had decided to begin having everyone telework. During the two weeks prior, there were a few symptomatic people who had come into the office. He decided to be cautious and get tested when he developed a cough. He informed his office mates and was not met with well wishes. Even though there had been people showing up to work with symptoms for weeks, the fact that he decided to get tested made him a target. The other people had excused themselves by explaining away their symptoms, saying it was allergies or a cold, but they really didn't know. Sure, regular colds and the flu did not cease to exist during this time, but it was still early for allergy season. His symptoms were less severe than those of others in his office.

In hindsight, he would have chosen to not disclose his choice to get tested to his coworkers. One man flipped out on the group message and stated, "We have families" before demanding to be removed from the correspondence. Another was more reasonable and stated that he had felt ill for a few days and did not realize that testing was available. When testing first came to our region, it was a lot harder to schedule. There was a tent site that had just opened up behind one of the hospitals. Most people simply ignored the message. There was only one man that reached out to him a few days later to ask how he was doing. His test results came back negative five days later.

There were only four confirmed positive staff in my building at this point. I was embarrassed at the thought of being one of only a few. I had been unmasked in my office and morning report daily and worried that others would blame me if they were to come down with the illness. I was not providing direct care and had not been doing unnecessary resident visits, mostly due to the lack of PPE. Because my job did not involve close physical contact with residents, I was afraid that people would assume that I had been irresponsible outside of work by continuing to go out and socialize. I chose to wear my mask in morning report and in the office that week. I informed my office mates and a few staff that I had been in close contact with during the week prior of my status. I stood out as the only person at the table wearing my mask, but people minded their business.

On test day, I was so nervous I couldn't eat lunch. Mark decided to come with me even though having others in the car was discouraged for their own safety. We had the conversation about social distancing many times. We live in a one-bedroom apartment together. I considered getting a hotel room if there was one available. I had also considered staying with a friend who had announced via social media weeks before that she had the virus. She had never been swabbed, but her primary care doctor had diagnosed her based off of symptoms alone. I'm relieved I never went with this option because she had antibody testing a few weeks after her illness and again a few months later and no antibodies were detected. We will revisit antibodies in greater detail in a moment. Mark took the stance that he would have been exposed already and chose not to change our life in any way.

We drove to the testing location, which was at one of the local college campuses. The hospital site had been very short-lived. There were big neon construction signs on the road pointing out where to go. When I pulled in with my face mask on, the police officer signaled me to roll up my car window and pull up. He told me through the window that the site had just shut down due to the weather. We pulled into a nearby parking lot and called the hotline to reschedule. I mentioned that I had already been scheduled and that the site had just been closed down. I was told that sometimes when the cancellation is due to the site closing, someone from the actual site would call those who missed appointments to reschedule. If not, I would have to go through the screening process again. I decided to wait a day and see if I would receive a call. I can't say I wasn't relieved. I was able to relax and go back home for lunch. I never did receive a call back about rescheduling. By the next day my sense of taste had started to return, so I never bothered going through the screening process again. There was a weird phase for a day or two when I could taste things but the flavors weren't quite right. I ate a Crunch bar and it tasted like coconut. I don't mind coconut flavor, but it's a disappointment when you're expecting chocolate.

I was pretty sure I had the virus because my loss of smell and taste were so bizarre. Usually when I lose these senses from a regular cold, it's because of a lot of congestion. This time it was not associated with any congestion. There were no other symptoms that stood out to me. I tried to think hard—did I maybe have a slight sore throat? Was I slightly more tired than the usual work-associated burnout feeling? This sounds ridiculous, but I decided to test myself. I went for a couple runs. I made sure to only run in areas where I could go very wide or cross streets to avoid passing by people. My thought was that if I had the virus, I would experience difficulties on a run. Maybe I would get short of breath or have trouble completing the miles. I became anxious before heading out that I might not be able to make it home. I considered bringing my phone, just in case, but decided to leave it at home. Working out during COVID-19 was uneventful. There were no changes in my cardiovascular ability.

There was a reason why I had this belief that I would struggle on a run. I mentioned the friend who had announced via social media weeks beforehand that she had the virus. The post was pretty dramatic, first broadcasting that she had the virus that week (even though there had never been a test to confirm). It then boasted about her prior athleticism and contrasted that with the current situation which was an inability to walk around the block post-virus. It ended like a public service announcement urging people to stay home and practice social distancing.

When I saw the post, I was both surprised and concerned. I called her immediately and was shocked to hear her car door opening. I was like, "Are you out in public?!" She said she wasn't infectious anymore because the fever occurred seventy-two hours beforehand and she was out running some errands. She was at the post office with plans to head over to the pharmacy next. During this brief conversation I heard her calling over a cat and she was petting it in the parking lot while we were talking. She suggested that we should hang out later if I wasn't busy, said she'd call back later, and excused herself to finish her outing.

This triggered my first strong emotional response related to the pandemic. I was terrified that she was out exposing vulnerable people to the illness. Whose cat was she petting? Was it going to be curled up on an eighty-year-old's lap that afternoon? This woman has a master's degree and her work often involved recognizing potential exposures. On some level, she must have understood that she was picking and choosing which pieces of the CDC's self-isolating guidelines to follow.

And unnecessary social visits were not recommended at this time regardless of one's health status. Knowing that someone with over a decade of public health experience was behaving in this manner made me feel like containing the virus would be impossible.

I was always concerned about the disease affecting vulnerable people. But the only reason I ever had a fear about the effects it might have on me were related to this dramatic story by someone my own age. If a self-proclaimed runner my age could no longer walk around the block, what would happen if I got the virus? Imagining a life immobilized was terrifying. So as much as I liked to think that I was well informed and rational, my beliefs were also influenced by unsubstantiated stories. But like the majority of cases in healthy people, I was basically asymptomatic. I tested positive for the antibodies a few weeks later.

A few months later, I developed some itchy bumps around my ankles. I first noticed them a day or two after we had grilled outside on a very buggy night, so I assumed they were bug bites. Over the next week the bumps turned into dried, raised patches and hard, pointy blisters. An area developed behind my left thigh and there were a few isolated bumps on my right forearm and right index finger. It became apparent that I had developed a sensitivity to poison ivy. I have always been one of the small percentage of people who is not affected by the plant. I've traipsed through the stuff my entire life. Our land has many "problem areas," and while Mark would wear boots and coveralls while working in these areas, I would always be comfortable in shorts and sandals.

People can develop a sensitivity to poison ivy at any point in their lives, however I couldn't help but think there may be a connection between the timing of my COVID-19 infection and the onset. Was it just a coincidence or was there a link? I reached out to a doctor friend for a professional medical opinion. It turned out she had been seeing this type of thing a lot. COVID-19 appears to make the immune system overly active for a time after the infection. One of her patients even had to be put on a daily antihistamine and inhaler. She recommended being cautious around common allergens for a while. Since the disease is so new, the long-term health effects are largely unknown. While the timing of my COVID-19 infection and onset of poison ivy sensitivity is most likely a coincidence, I blame the disease for taking away my superpower.

Chapter 6: PPE or Lack Thereof

The most frustrating part of the PPE situation was the lack of communication. In the beginning, I believe this was because the facility was not able to provide adequate protection for their staff, so upper-level management stayed vague about the procedures rather than admitting to staff they were being blatantly put in harm's way with no hazard pay. The hazard pay topic had been brought up in morning report once by Chad after he had been approached by several aides about it. At the time there were no confirmed cases of COVID-19 in the building, so he justified not providing hazard pay by the fact that none of the staff were working around the disease. When the illness was confirmed to be rampant in the building, the topic was brushed off.

At this time, it is unclear whether or not COVID-19 has an airborne route of transmission versus only droplets. Droplets are larger particles that generally do not travel very far or stay in the air as long. The flu is an example of a virus that is spread primarily via droplets. Airborne transmission, on the other hand, is when much smaller particles become aerosolized, and it requires more strict precautions. Many hospitals dealing with people carrying an illness that has an airborne route of transmission will place the person in an isolation room with negative pressure if possible. Measles and chicken pox are a couple of examples of illnesses with a known airborne route of transmission.

When we were first required to wear surgical masks in the building, there was a severe shortage. We were instructed to save our masks for a week at a time. This was a disgusting situation even for staff like myself, who spent the majority of their working day at a computer in an office where it was acceptable to take the mask off. After a couple of uses, you can usually smell your own saliva. Staff became mindful of what they ate for lunch because they did not want to risk smelling it for several days afterward. Most agreed that tuna fish sandwiches were not a good option during this time.

These surgical masks were of varying quality. My first mask was yellow and fit pretty nicely. When I noticed one day that the staff entrance had been recently stocked with blue masks, I was excited to toss the old one for a fresh one. I quickly regretted this decision when I realized that the wire piece that you shape over your nose only extended through about half of the mask. Consequently, it fit poorly and would ride up and poke me in the eye repeatedly. Amanda somehow scored a box of white surgical masks which we hid in our office for a time.

There was also a problem with the reliability of the entrances being stocked with the needed masks. The front door was always stocked. This was the door through which corporate and theoretically the DOH would enter the building, if they were to come. Both of these groups were safely teleworking during this time.

However, the staff entrance was more often than not completely out of the surgical masks. It only took one or two embarrassing trips through the building with my shirt pulled up over my mouth and nose before I learned to not throw my mask out at the end of the day. Even if it was getting disgusting, it was best to hang onto it to wear in for the trip through the building to the main entrance the next day.

There was very little talk about the use of N95 respirators. I don't know when the topic was officially discussed, because it was not during morning report. The only way to obtain one was to request one through the infectious disease nurse. We had weekly wound meetings, usually in the early afternoon on Fridays. Usually the most reliable of the unit managers and I would be waiting in the conference room for up to an hour past the agreed upon time for the meeting to start. We would bring our laptops and use this time to catch up on documentation. On one occasion, there were a few of us waiting and one of the nurses brought in a box of N95s, which had been donated by a neighbor with a nice greeting card offering encouragement and thanking us for our hard work. The HR lady's office is just off the conference room, and she could not help but come in to see what we were up to due to the secretive nature of the transaction taking place. We each took an N95 respirator to hide for personal use. We were afraid that we would be caught in the act when Pam, the ADON and infectious disease nurse, finally showed up to begin the meeting. What we were doing felt more scandalous than passing around drug paraphernalia. I still have that perfect N95 saved in a desk drawer.

The N95 respirators are more protective for the user than a surgical mask, however, they are most effective when the user has been fit tested to ensure that there are no leaks. Even during my dietetic internship, I had been fit tested in order to visit with certain patients in the hospital. Only six nurses were chosen to be fit tested at our facility, and it was well after the disease had spread around. These were the nurses who would be administering the nasopharyngeal swabs when regular COVID-19 staff testing in nursing homes was mandated by the state.

Hand sanitizer was a little tricky too. Before the pandemic, doomsday preppers and survivalist types were seen as weirdos. I think it has become a little more mainstream now, or at least a temporary fad during our times. In my twenties, I completed some long-distance hiking trails, including the 2190-mile Appalachian Trail, which runs from Georgia to Maine. I would not consider myself a prepper, but I have an interest and experience in self-sufficiency and survival skills. My dad bought me a *Prepper* magazine a couple years back for my birthday. The articles featured survival strategies for a variety of disaster scenarios. I enjoyed it, so Mark decided to put together an emergency "go kit" that year for Christmas. The kit contained N95 respirators and several small bottles of hand sanitizer, so I felt lucky when these things became scarce. The reasoning behind the go kit N95s was more to provide protection from inhaling smoke particles during forest fires (Mark is from California). They have also come in handy while helping family members clean up basements filled with mold and pet waste.

The little hand sanitizer bottles met the minimum alcohol percentage requirement recommended by the CDC so they were adequate, but not as good as the medical grade stuff in the facility. I made the comment that I was starting to run low and would need to remember to bring in another bottle sometime within the next couple days. Meg has seniority over almost everyone in the building and has a "time in service" award made of glass on her desk to show for it. She also has a very low tolerance for bullshit. She walked over to the central supply office and scored me a large bottle of hand sanitizer. Despite her seniority, she was met with opposition. She was told that if I needed hand sanitizer, I could get some myself. This was annoying given the fact that the week prior I had driven almost two hours round trip to pick up tube feeding supplies for a resident due to an oversight in the central supply office.

Gowns were also in short supply. When COVID-19 was grudgingly acknowledged to be in the building, the use of gowns became necessary. There were stations just outside of each of the units, which served as staging areas for changing into and out of your gown. Most of the gowns were reusable. Gallon-sized plastic bags and Sharpies were located at the station so that you could label and stash your bagged gown in a plastic tote in this area. These were the gowns that you had to wear just to go onto the unit. There were also gowns hung on the inside of rooms with COVID-19 positive residents or new admits/suspected exposures. These gowns were dedicated for the residents, not the staff. So, staff had to share the same gown while working with these patients until the gown became visibly soiled or damaged. This was a very stressful time with staffing shortages, so staff were working hard and sweating while sharing these gowns.

No gowns were to be worn off the units. My office mates arrived for their day around six o'clock and seven fifteen. I do not have the discipline to go to bed early enough to support that kind of schedule. When I arrived that day at eight thirty, my usual time, I walked into a cloud of disinfectant spray. One of the CNAs (certified nursing assistants) had walked into our office fully gowned to tell Amanda something nonurgent. Meg was livid that she had been super careful throughout the pandemic only to have an entitled aide come into her office in a contaminated gown.

It was during this time that I stopped going on wound rounds. When the gown situation started, I bowed out to save PPE for the necessary participants. Dietitians joining in on the wound rounds is a bit of an old-school practice, but I enjoy it when I have time because it's fascinating and also helps to be able to visualize the healing process and speak directly with the wound doctors. Most wounds require daily care, but they also need to be tracked and measured more closely weekly by the doctor or at least a wound RN to be sure the interventions in place are still working. During a perfect wound round, the aides would have the resident positioned and the wounds unwrapped right before the doctor comes to the unit. The doctor then takes the measurements and may do a treatment or suggest changes to the current wound care routine. The aides and/or LPNs then follow behind and dress the wound. Wound rounds NEVER run this smoothly. Oftentimes the resident isn't even in their room. The aides mysteriously disappear and the doctors complain that they will be late to the next facility.

For some reason, I have a strong stomach when it comes to wounds. I have seen recent amputations, gangrenous toes, bleeding diabetic ulcers, and deep pressure injuries. Sometimes the wounds can have a strong odor. The wound doctor will occasionally whip out a little scalpel and start debriding the wound. This means that they are removing the dead tissue. They can also do this chemically. One of the coolest treatments involves a chemical debridement applied by what looks like matchsticks. Another process frequently seen on wound rounds is the packing of deep and tunneling pressure injuries with gauze. Pressure injuries are of particular interest to the dietitian because they require extra protein and sometimes a vitamin/mineral supplement to help with healing. These wounds are staged based on severity.

The term "pressure injury" means the same thing as a pressure ulcer. An expert advisory panel updated the terminology and staging back in 2016; however, the nursing homes I've worked in seem to always be way behind the times. Another example of an outdated practice, the continued use of which is still the norm, is unclogging a feeding tube with soda. This can create a worse clog by causing a reaction with the tube feed formula and can also degrade the tubing material. The best way to fix the problem is to use enzymes such as CREON to dissolve the clog. CREON is a medicine used by people with pancreatic insufficiency. It's basically digestive enzymes for people who cannot produce their own. It's expensive, so nursing homes are not in a hurry to start using it for another purpose. The nurses just learn not to mention the soda method in front of the dietitian unless they are bored and want to get me a little animated during a meeting.

The wound doctors with whom I've worked are outsourced like myself. They commonly have a surgical background and travel to multiple facilities. The first doctor I worked with at Dutch Meadows was an amiable man with a full schedule. He serviced ten facilities and therefore could not afford to miss one or else it was impossible to make it up within the week. This doctor was a bit of a germaphobe. When I had worked with him previously at Falls View, I would amuse myself by reporting to him the outbreaks of norovirus and the flu on different units. He would be noticeably uncomfortable as he gloved up. I wondered how he had made it in the medical field. I worked with him for several months at Falls View and unfortunately was only able to join him for a few rounds at Dutch Meadows before the virus hit. He did not come in after our first residents tested positive in the hospital. Apparently, he was able to continue on with the other facilities with nurses using a tablet or cell phone so that he could visualize the wound and advise on treatment remotely. This was not acceptable to Dutch Meadows, so another male doctor from his company replaced him. His service was short-lived because his company had a policy that once there was active COVID-19 in the building, the doctor could not come in because he serviced multiple buildings.

Their company policy was probably a good idea, because the surgeon who replaced him tested positive for COVID-19 a week after starting and was out for the two-week quarantine. I had also worked with this doctor in the past. I rounded with her at Arbor Park. She was still working as a surgeon and therefore did not service as many facilities as the others. She was a marathon runner and was completely asymptomatic when she tested positive with the virus.

The facility doctor had some interesting ideas regarding the PPE shortage. He suggested staff bring in their bathrobes and snorkeling goggles. These ideas were laughed off, but writing this much later, I think the goggles would have been helpful. Eye protection was never something offered at the facility throughout the outbreak; now it's recognized as standard. Bringing in bathrobes from home would have been a little awkward, though. Who would have laundered them? Would we have been expected to bring the contaminated bathrobe home daily or leave it at the facility to be cleaned? I don't feel it would have been appreciated if I brought in my bathrobe advertising a nudie event. The other one is long and plush and would have been too warm to wear around for long. Even that one is from Victoria's Secret, which might be a little too risqué.

Chapter 7: The Worst Week

This week was the period of time during which there was a drastic drop in our census. There were so many people leaving for the hospital and not returning that we were down from around 130 residents to less than eighty. I typically go for a daily walk after lunch, but I started to feel uneasy when returning to the facility because I wouldn't know what to expect. Oftentimes there would be ambulances lined up at the front door. I would hear sirens in the distance or see the ambulances drive by and know they were going to my workplace. On the worst day, there was a fleet of half a dozen that had showed up during my thirty-minute escape.

The EMTs would often litter the parking lot with their gloves on the way out rather than dispose of them properly, which added to the post-apocalyptic atmosphere. I left work one day at the same time a medical crew was arriving to pick up a resident. The level of PPE they were wearing shocked me. The way I described this outfit to Mark was that it looked like a beekeeping suit with a motor attached to the back of a belt. He informed me that it sounded like a PAPR (powered air-purifying respirator). It's an interesting feeling walking around in the same environment with someone wearing a PAPR when all you have on is a flimsy surgical mask.

On Wednesday, April 22nd, a female resident (9) in her fifties went out to the hospital and tested positive for the virus. The first documentation of her having fever/chills was in the early morning two weeks prior. By the afternoon, she had increased lethargy. She was started on Bactrim for a UTI a few days later. There were no lab results available to indicate that she tested positive for bacteria in her urine. The fever resolved until a couple weeks later when she spiked a high fever and showed signs of dehydration. This was when she was sent to the hospital, where she stayed for six weeks. She attempted to return to the facility, but she was not herself, and fell immediately upon her return and went right back out with a bloody nose and involuntary lip-smacking movements. We received her COVID-19 results from the hospital, which indicated she was still testing positive. She returned to us for good five days later. At no point during her illness did she have any respiratory symptoms. She made a full recovery.

We learned of positive results from four other residents who were tested in-house on the same day the previous resident left for her first hospital stay. An eighty-year-old woman (12) initially had a general complaint of not feeling well. She had only been in the facility for ten days and was therefore on the unit with all the others on contact precautions. She became lethargic with poor meal intakes and hypotension, and was started on IV fluids. She was approached about COVID-19 testing and was in agreement. She was moved off the contact precautions unit once she had been there for two weeks to make room for more admissions. This move happened before receiving the test results even though she had been symptomatic. She had already been with her new roommate for days when we received the positive results. Her symptoms had resolved by this point.

A woman in her early seventies was reported to have an upset stomach and loose stools over the previous two days. She also had a harsh, dry cough, poor appetite, sore throat, irritated eyes, and shortness of breath. A few days later it was noted, "continues on azithromycin." However, there was no previous documentation to explain when and why this antibiotic was started. She did receive a chest X-ray which showed negative for acute disease. And upon writing this, I realized this was not one of the residents who tested positive on that day. It was someone who shared the same last name as that resident. I decided to keep it in the story as an example of just how many people were symptomatic and how arbitrarily our facility doled out the tests at this point in time. I added her to my nowhere-near-exhaustive list of probable cases.

The actual COVID-positive resident from that day was a male in his mid-seventies (11). He spiked a low-grade fever with complaints of a stomach ache and cough. No cough was heard by staff members. He was started on a Z-Pak (Zithromax) for five days along with prednisone. Nurses attempted to collect a stool sample to test for C. diff. He was also approached about changing units on this day. A few days later he was tested for COVID-19 with positive results. He reported that he had no appetite and was very tired. A chest X-ray had been ordered days prior and was still not completed.

The lab was called and reported that they were behind and would be going to our facility ASAP. There was no documentation of it ever being completed before he was sent to the hospital with SOB and O2 saturation of 76 percent. He never returned to the facility.

A man in his late fifties (10) had a timeline almost identical to that of resident eleven (11). He was approached about testing, was agreeable, and received positive results. He had also moved units on the same day. There were two massive resident moves during the outbreak. This was the first one, which occurred before it was confirmed that a lot of these residents were already positive. There was the same issue with the follow-through of the chest X-ray order, and although he never left the facility, there was no documentation that it ever happened. He was asymptomatic throughout the entire illness. He was married and his wife also lived in the facility at the time. They had ordered pizza a week beforehand and enjoyed the meal and some kisses out in the lobby. Ten days later, he consoled his wife from across the hallway because she was distraught about going to the ER. He made a full recovery, but she passed away at the end of May. She had not been on my suspected cases list, but our social worker was convinced that she had COVID-19. And the timeline makes sense.

The last of the positive cases on this Wednesday was a woman in her early sixties (13). She first spiked a fever, then had complaints of congestion, a cough, and weakness in her legs. She was flushed and weak and had a fall during this time. She was started on Levoquin for an upper respiratory infection (URI). She had increased dyspnea (difficulty breathing) and was hypoxic (low oxygen in blood). She went to the hospital and passed away. When my coworkers talk about surprising deaths from COVID-19, they usually bring up this woman as an example. They thought she was relatively healthy and young and did not think that it would take her, of all people.

That Friday, the facility sent six residents to the hospital. Five out of six tested positive. I felt that the woman who tested negative was a false negative. I don't think false negatives happened often, but she almost certainly fell into that category. She may have gone out for testing and returned without being admitted because there was no gap in her documentation. She was on IV antibiotics for an infection in her knee and was occasionally non-compliant with the treatment because it made her nauseous. Four days later, she was put on another antibiotic for a URI. A productive cough and low-grade fever were noted. We had a care conference in person with her on this date. The documentation stated that she declined to attend, but she was present. She may have initially declined and then decided she felt well enough at the last moment and wheeled herself there. She had a poor appetite at the time, but there was nothing that indicated to me that she would not make progress and return home fairly soon. She had a suspected stroke and passed away in the hospital.

The first of the positives from that day was a woman (14) who had frequent falls. She had a pretty significant one and was noted to have a laceration on the back of her head. She was extremely agitated on that day, refused monitoring of her vital signs, and only accepted a few bites of her lunch. The restlessness and confusion continued, and she had more falls over the next few days. She was showing signs of pain. She was transferred out to the hospital because of her overall decline. She tested positive in the hospital and never returned to the facility. Her family was very upset with the facility and refused to allow her to return.

Falls are a very difficult situation for nursing facilities to manage, especially when residents are noncompliant or may be so confused that they keep trying to stand up and walk even if they don't have that ability anymore. There are very strict rules against using restraints of any kind (chemical or physical) and the reasons for these rules are common sense. An example of a chemical restraint would be a psychoactive medication, which is determined to be for staff convenience more than for the benefit of a resident. These facilities are becoming responsible for an increasing number of psych patients and the staff is usually not trained to deal with these types of patients. De-escalating a violent patient requires skill and time (both of which are lacking in this setting). Staff oftentimes deal with being kicked, slapped, spit on, or worse as part of their everyday routine. Having seen the effects of human bites, I understand the appeal of chemical restraints. A physical restraint is an object or device that the individual cannot remove easily which restricts freedom of movement or normal access to one's body. Something as simple as a wheelchair belt or bed rails can be considered physical restraints depending on the situation.

The falls and violent incidents are exactly the type of things that are covered daily at the end of morning report when the incidents and accidents (I&As) are reviewed. For every single one there must be documentation showing that something was done to prevent the same event from recurring. When there is a resident who is constantly getting up and moving around, it gets very tricky and staff have to be creative. That is why every clinical discipline is involved. For example, the dietitian could theoretically come in handy if there is a suspected blood sugar issue involved or someone is food seeking at night. And when I say staff sometimes need to get creative, I really mean it. While definitely not the oddest intervention put in place, an interesting one that comes to mind was the time we had a woman who was developing a pressure injury because she held onto a baby doll all day long. The solution was to clothe the doll a little better so that there weren't hard parts digging into the woman's skin.

The second positive that Friday was a woman in her mid-eighties (15) who spent a lot of her time in the activities room. She had dementia and was pleasantly confused. I would often see her on my way out. One day she asked me, "Why is everyone wearing masks? Are there a lot of sick people?" I told her that the staff were wearing masks since we come in from outside and we don't want to bring in our germs. There was no protocol regarding what we told residents about the pandemic. She may have been one of the residents who became agitated by the masks at times. When someone is already confused and used to certain people and a routine, it is very stressful when they can't recognize those people. She started to have a poor appetite and was sleeping for longer intervals. She was feeling generally unwell and then became confused and had loose stools. There was an occasional dry cough noted toward the end of her time at the facility. Her oxygen saturation dropped, and she went to the ER, where her family requested a trial intubation. It was unsuccessful.

The third positive was a man in his early eighties (16) who was started on antibiotics for a URI. His appetite was starting to become variable around this time. He had a fall earlier in the month, which resulted in a broken hip and weeklong stay in the hospital. An experienced healthcare worker once told me that a broken hip is oftentimes the beginning of the end for seniors. It certainly was for this gentleman, possibly because he may have contracted the virus while in the hospital. He became increasingly tired and confused. He was started on clysis. Fluid resuscitation did not help in this case. His mental status and responsiveness continued to decline and he was sent to the hospital. He passed away.

The fourth positive was a seventy-seven-year-old man (17) who had a fall a couple days before developing symptoms. It began with complaints of body aches, cough, a poor appetite, and lethargy. He was feeling SOB with exertion. He had irregular lab results and went out to the hospital for almost two months. Three months later, he had not returned to baseline. He was very sleepy and unable to participate in most therapy sessions. There seemed to be some cognitive impairment as well. For example, he would have an empty bowl in front of him and continue moving his arm with a spoon in his hand between the bowl and his mouth.

The last of the positives sent out that Friday was a woman in her mid-seventies (18). The week before our first known case, she was flushed and spiked a fever. She had a room change to another wing two weeks prior. There were multiple notes related to increased agitation and yelling out over the next few days. This was assumed to be due to the move, and then her appetite decreased a few days later. Then wheezing was noted. Psych meds were withheld due to lethargy. The next day she was sent to the hospital when her oxygen saturation dropped to 89 percent on 4L of oxygen. She returned a few days later. She was transferred back out almost a month later for decreasing oxygen levels again and congestion, which she may have been able to clear if she had the cognitive ability to follow the doctor's instructions. She returned again after only a couple of days in the hospital. Karen, the DON, felt that the hospital kept sending her back too quickly due to her behavior.

Her case was a very sad one. This woman had been in a successful career. She went out for a surgery which should have been routine and had a stroke which put her in a permanent dementia-like state. She yelled out for hours at a time and would even break a sweat from getting herself so worked up. Her sisters insisted on keeping her full code—meaning all measures had to be taken to prolong her life, even at the expense of her comfort. This limited the facility's ability to make her comfortable.

Some family members feel that this is the morally correct thing to do. This can frustrate nursing, especially in cases when the family rarely even stays in touch. The nurse may know the resident more intimately than the family member who is legally appointed to make their medical decisions. If someone with full code status is found unresponsive, the nurse is required to perform CPR. This is traumatic for both the nurse and the patient if the procedure is successful. It is not like what you see in a movie. People who have performed CPR can never unhear the sound of ribs breaking.

The next two residents were among the many obvious COVID-19 cases, which were never confirmed with a test. The doctor had gone through the building during the onset of the outbreak and encouraged certain residents to downgrade their code status. He coerced many of the residents that he did not consider "viable" to change from full code to DNR (do not resuscitate) and/or DNH (do not hospitalize). The DNH residents were the easiest to get away with because the facility did not even have to worry about these residents turning up positive from the routine testing at the hospital. These residents were never tested and therefore were "freebies" for the facility. Many residents who were very obvious COVID-19 cases were never tested for the illness and were therefore never counted in the statistics. Most of the ones of which I am aware of died.

On the same day that the six were sent out to the hospital, a woman in her mid-seventies was noted to have slightly labored breathing and her color was very pale. She was in and out of responsiveness and died on this day. She had chronic obstructive pulmonary disease (COPD) and required oxygen, however there was no documentation to indicate that there was anything wrong with her leading up to her death except for a note the day before indicating that she "continued" on Levaquin and a Z-Pak. This is another example of this wording being used even when the resident is just starting on antibiotic therapy. Oftentimes, an antibiotic appeared in a resident's progress notes with no valid explanation as to why it had been started. Antibiotics are used for bacterial infections. COVID-19, like a cold or the flu, is a virus which cannot be cured with an antibiotic. Since the virus was spreading around the facility, a COVID-19 test should have been the first order considered for any sick resident. Rather, residents were started on an antibiotic for a urinary tract infection or upper respiratory infection, usually without lab results to support that diagnosis.

A man who was the exact same age as the previous resident and also on supplemental oxygen died three days later. He did, however, have a documented decline leading up to his death. His intakes were poor all through the month. He had loose stools for a few days. He received IV fluids. A urine sample came back negative for a UTI. However, a week later he was noted to be taking antibiotics for a UTI. He had difficulty breathing, which started within a week. He had an occasional cough with congestion. He had increasing confusion and began persistently calling out for various people. The names were presumably those of family members. Staff attempted to calm him, but he would start back up once they left the room. He died on April 27th.

A chest X-ray was ordered by the doctor for a man in his upper fifties (19) because he had had an intermittent fever over the previous few days, along with abnormal chest sounds. The results came back negative for acute disease. He was then offered a COVID-19 test. He asked if a positive result could affect his discharge, which was planned for the following week, and was told that it was a possibility. He initially declined for this reason. After a long discussion with his sister, he agreed to take the test, and it came back positive on April 25th. It was noted that he had a room change a few days later at his request. Once moved, he became shaky and short of breath, and turned blue. The staff was unable to obtain an accurate oxygen saturation reading and he went out to the hospital. I never learned of his fate; however, I do know that there was one resident who had a planned return to the facility and passed away en route the day he was to return. This may or may not have been him.

Another man in his early eighties (27) was on antibiotics to treat an abscess. His decreased appetite was the first noticeable symptom. He ate less than 50 percent of his meals one day and complained of severe back pain. A couple of days later, he had a hacking cough. He was lying in bed moaning because of body aches and an upset stomach. He was pale and sweaty. A few days later, his oxygen saturation was around 80 percent. The NP (nurse practitioner) ordered a chest X-ray and additional antibiotics. The following morning, a new order was placed for IV fluids, which he received with no issues. He started having increased difficulty breathing while lying flat. By then he had a change in condition and requested to go to the hospital. His request was granted despite the fact that he was a DNR/DNH with no health care proxy to inform. This was a good move because he made a full recovery and returned to us a month later. He had tested positive in the hospital.

We were not the only facility in the area to be hit by the pandemic. Around this time, a friend at another facility texted me a chart from a news article that came out about the COVID-19 status of local nursing homes. The chart contained separate columns for the number of residents and staff at each facility who tested positive. My friend's facility had higher numbers than the one where I worked. She worked at a very highly rated nursing home where all residents have private rooms. She told me that once one of their nurse managers tested positive, everyone on that unit was automatically tested, staff and residents. There was also a facility run by the state which was on the top of the list. This facility, along with some private expensive places, were most featured in the news because of their transparency and responsible testing practices. The virus did not affect these places at a higher rate or spread more quickly.

Chapter 8: A Steady Rate of Cases

There was a period of about a month when the drama slowed down and there was a steady rate of cases discovered from different sources. Even after the recent abundance of cases and deaths in the facility, there was no facility testing during this time because there was nobody forcing the hand of corporate to do so. A very heavyset man with several comorbidities went out to the hospital and tested positive (28) on Friday, May 1st. He stayed out for almost a month before returning. He was put on therapy and worked for about three months before reaching a plateau in progress. Although he progressed, he was not back to baseline a full four months later.

On Saturday, May 2nd, another dialysis patient (20) tested positive. He had very mild symptoms, especially considering his comorbidities. Although the dialysis patients had been moved to the rehab unit early on to contain people going out into the community, nothing changed regarding the procedure for how they went out for their triweekly treatments. All residents were quarantined on their units at this point, but the dialysis patients still came out to the lobby to wait for their rides. This dialysis patient refused to wear a mask at one point. This was a resident who had always been a fan of wearing masks for his own protection.

One day, Chad stated that obese people are 50 percent more likely to die from COVID-19. The two gentlemen just mentioned met the criteria for the morbid obesity diagnosis. There are a lot of statistics substantiating how obesity and various comorbidities relate to COVID-19. Both of these men survived. They both had significant other comorbidities as well. They were perfect examples of why we can't generalize and try to guess one's likelihood of survival.

I had a care conference with a very likeable man in his mid-seventies (21) the same week. The SLP (speech and language pathologist) invited me in for a diabetes management lesson during one of her sessions so that she could continue working with him on the material during their cognition sessions. After we worked with him, I noticed that COVID-19 was listed under his medical diagnoses. What was interesting about his case was that he was not tested for the virus. Considering that there were so many symptomatic people not tested or diagnosed by symptoms, I'm not sure why his case was different. The diagnosis has since been removed from the list. He's the one person on my positive list who may not have actually had the illness.

A resident who relied completely on tube feeding (23) went out to the hospital and tested positive on May 7th. His wife liked to keep in contact every day, and many staff considered her to be a nuisance, but her observations were always spot-on. If she felt that there was something going on with her husband, there was a legitimate concern. She regularly had Zoom meetings with him. One time she conveniently was stepping out of the shower at a time she had scheduled a video chat. She said, "Look, John, a naked lady." The staff member running the call was also treated to the full-frontal nudity.

Another man (22) went out to the hospital and tested positive on the same day as the man with the lively wife. He was one of those who frequented the dining room after it was technically shut down. His illness began with a decrease in appetite, which was very unusual for him. He was always eager for his next meal or snack. This gentleman was very sociable and enjoyed staff attention. So, when he started requesting assistance with meals, some of the nursing staff suspected that he may have been jealous of his roommate, who had been declining at the time. He spiked a fever and quickly developed a cough with SOB. He was flushed and his oxygen levels started dropping. He went out to the hospital and our staff were relieved to receive an update from the hospital that he was his old self, flirting with all the nurses.

He was at the hospital for nearly three weeks. When he returned, his appetite was still not good. Part of the problem was that he had lost a lot of his swallowing ability and needed a mechanically altered diet and thickened liquids. He continued to lose weight in the facility because he didn't like the pureed food. The SLP was able to advance his diet a little, but he never returned to his baseline consumption of regular textures and liquids. He did, however, get used to the ground/cut meals and nectar thick liquids. He looked forward to mealtimes again and gained the weight back.

Another dialysis resident (30) went out to the hospital and tested positive around the same time. What was really frustrating about his case was that he probably did not need to be in the facility as long as he had been. The director of social work and director of therapy had an ongoing rivalry, and there was some disagreement about his discharge date. Theoretically, he could have gone home earlier and been subjected to the hot zone for a much shorter period of time. This man was very interesting and had authored several books in two languages. His long-term plan was to sell his home in New York and spend the rest of his days abroad. He did recover and return home to start implementing this plan. Unfortunately, this was short-lived. He was not able to care for himself in the home and returned to the facility in poor condition. He had lost weight and had a serious fall with fractures. After-effects of the virus may have contributed to his sharp decline. He has since died.

We briefly had a resident receiving total parenteral nutrition (24) (TPN). This means that almost all of her nutrition and hydration needs were met with intravenous feedings. Our facility had just spent some time getting ready to receive these patients regularly. She was our first. These patients are actually managed through a nutrition support service offered through the pharmacy that compounds the solution for the feedings. I had worked with their dietitians previously at Falls View and enjoyed having these specialists collaborating with me and doing all of the high-pressure work calculating the orders with their pharmacist. Sometimes I would be a little embarrassed having to try to explain some of the shortcomings of these facilities. The service provided some training to the nursing staff on TPN administration. Unfortunately, this resident was not there long before contracting the virus, going out to the hospital, and passing away. I did not find out about her fate until months later when I asked admissions. We have not had any other TPN residents since. I'm assuming it was determined to be a little too much to handle during the pandemic.

Around this time, a lot of our administrative staff were out sick. Pam, Karen, and Chad were all out at the same time. The two nurses were tested for COVID-19 and returned to work after receiving negative results. They were out for about a week. Chad refused to get tested. Instead, he went to a family member who was a gynecologist for antibody testing. He returned to work very symptomatic on a Thursday, which was the day we had meetings that lasted all morning. He took up his place at the head of the table. There were more people than usual in the conference room on meeting days, so he had people sitting within two feet of him. He removed his mask, coughed, and touched his face throughout the meeting. One of the people seated right next to him was Sue, who had a persistent smoker's cough. She felt that she was at high risk because of her respiratory status. I was livid after this event and put in complaints with both OSHA and the New York State Department of Labor (DOL). My specific complaints were related to symptomatic staff coming to work without being tested for the illness and no enforcement of masking and social distancing in required staff meetings. Nothing happened as a result of either.

On May 11th, another one of our dialysis patients (25) tested positive. This was a very young man who unfortunately had lived, and continued to live, a very rough life. He had many health problems as a result. He was asymptomatic for quite a while after his diagnosis. Then his meal intakes declined because the illness affected his taste. He complained that everything tasted sour. He was sent to the emergency room about a week after his diagnosis and did not have an easy time in the hospital. He was there for weeks and on a ventilator, but he pulled through and returned to the facility.

COVID-19 did not take this man directly, but most likely indirectly led to his death. For quite some time, staff had suspected that he was buying drugs while out at dialysis appointments. He was searched upon returning from these appointments. But residents are always able to sneak things into facilities. He had C. diff and it was suspected that he may have hidden contraband in his briefs where nobody would check. He had been spotted meeting people outside of the dialysis facility, where he would go down the road and behind some trees out of direct line of sight. A unit manager had come up with a simple solution—changing his dialysis time to earlier in the day. Appointments can start earlier than six a.m. The manager said, "Ain't no drug dealer out that early." I thought it was a fantastic idea! Unfortunately, it wasn't implemented quickly enough, and he died unexpectedly of a suspected drug overdose. A coworker pointed out that he most likely detoxed while in the hospital and then tried to take the same amount of drug that he took prior to his hospitalization.

A woman in her late eighties (31) had not been in the facility a full month. She had a lot of GI issues during her stay, which may have been explained by antibiotic therapy for sepsis. She abruptly started having trouble breathing and her oxygen levels dropped. She was sent to the hospital and died.

At the same time, a dialysis patient in his mid-sixties (26) started feeling generally unwell. He had episodes of confusion where he knew who he was but not where he was or current events. Dialysis sent him to the emergency room, where he tested positive for COVID-19 and returned to the facility. The next day, nursing had trouble maintaining his oxygen saturation even with supplemental oxygen. He was very confused and lethargic. He went back to the hospital and he, also, passed away.

I found out about a case (29) originating from our facility from an unexpected source. A woman who had stayed at the facility posted on a social media page. This page normally directed its negative energy toward Falls View, but a friend working at that facility found this post. This woman had been at Dutch Meadows a little less than a week. A few days into her stay, she spiked a temperature. She was given Tylenol and her fever came down a little. The NP (nurse practitioner) and infectious disease nurse were notified and were monitoring her fever. There were no documented fevers for the remainder of her short stay. I would have forgotten about her entirely had it not been for my friend discovering her post. It began with her stating that the only thing she gained from the facility was

COVID-19. Therefore, she must have had further symptoms after her stay which prompted her to seek testing after being discharged. This made sense because she was at the facility during the sketchy denial period when the virus was allowed to spread around the building unchecked. She further commented on the infrequent cleaning in her room, inconsistent PPE use among staff, and rudeness among some staff toward residents who were unable to advocate for themselves.

A seventy-year-old male [33] had a fall one evening and the RN doing the fall assessment noted his temperature was 101.7. He had no other symptoms until three days later. He stated that he wasn't feeling well and lost his appetite. His mouth and lips were dry. A few days later, he was very fatigued and became incontinent, which was unusual for him. A urine sample was taken to check for a UTI. He vomited after lunch a few days later. He had a chest X-ray, which showed bilateral pulmonary infiltrates. He was put on antibiotics for the respiratory infection. A nurse was called to his room because his oxygen saturation dropped. She was able to bring it up to 90 percent with supplemental oxygen. He had vomited a large amount. Upon this resident's request, he was sent to the hospital. This was almost three weeks after the onset of symptoms. He spent two weeks in the hospital. COVID-19 had been added to his medical diagnoses list.

Before this gentleman became ill, there was a progress note about how one day a nurse came upon him crying hysterically. He was upset because he was being incessantly harassed by another male in his upper seventies. The man doing the teasing frequently mocks other residents, and whenever the staff calls him out on it, he always just says they were joking around. The other person is never in agreement. I don't know if they were roommates at the time, but this note made it obvious that the two had contact. This man fell ill and went through a very rough time shortly after the man he had been taunting went out to the hospital. This may have been how he was exposed, although there were many potential sources at that point. His oxygen started dropping significantly, and he kept taking off his oxygen mask. He no doubt had COVID-19, but he was a DNH, so if he had passed, he would have been another freebie. He is a freebie as far as positive reported cases. He recovered and is up to his usual antics.

I hadn't been able to really get to know a lot of my residents because of the questionable PPE situation. There were two women sharing a room in the rehab unit who had not had the illness, and I was eager to meet with them. I suited up and went over for a visit one afternoon. They were getting a little bored being stuck in the room all day and appreciated a chat. One of the women was a dialysis patient (34). She mentioned that she was a little tired because she had been up vomiting all night. She attributed it to the pizza her roommate had ordered and shared with her. I asked if she had issues with heartburn or if she had had this kind of reaction to pizza before. She had not. One of the nurse's aides wandered in at one point and a comment was made that indicated that nursing was aware of this resident's symptoms the night before. I documented it in the medical record and figured that nursing was already following the situation based on the aide's awareness. I should not have assumed anything, because there was no documentation in the chart about it before my assessment.

Three days later, the woman vomited again overnight and spiked a fever. The unit manager acted as if this was the first time she had been made aware of any symptoms. Because she was a dialysis patient, the facility would not be able to get away with as much. She adamantly refused to go to the hospital. During my conversation with her a few days prior, she had gone on an emotional tangent about how she was okay with the idea of death. She was not suicidal or even depressed, but she was at peace and had her end of life plans in order.

She complained of pain in her mid-back, which worsened. She was started on two antibiotics for the fever and possible URI. The note literally stated this reason. She developed a cough and slight congestion. A chest X-ray was ordered and came back negative. She went to dialysis the next day and was sent out to the hospital from there to test for COVID-19 and for further evaluation due to her change in condition. While at dialysis, her oxygen saturation had dropped and she became short of breath. She was in the hospital for ten days. A progress note indicated that she tested positive in the hospital, but it was never added to her diagnoses. She was very overwhelmed by her illness when she first returned. She continued to have bouts of nausea and vomiting. She was never the same emotionally after her illness. She was distant, stressed, and not able to fully engage with others. She passed away a few months later.

Her roommate passed away, presumably of complications related to congestive heart failure. She was found unresponsive on the floor next to her bed. She was not always compliant with her medications, but this was nothing new. She had declined her weight checks, so it was unknown if she was overloaded with fluid. She had multiple complaints about insomnia and fatigue. Over a week before her sudden death, there was a progress note about pending COVID-19 test results. She was probably required to receive testing because of her roommate's status. There were never any results documented.

CHAPTER 9: STAFF TESTING

Around the second week in May, we started discussing the impending need for all nursing home staff to undergo regular COVID-19 testing. Chad was deathly afraid of the nasopharyngeal swab and paid close attention to any loopholes around the new rule. At first, any individual who had previously tested positive for the illness or who could provide documentation of a positive antibody test was exempt. Chad mentioned this clause in meetings; however, Pam was never on board with the antibody option.

I had been trying to find antibody testing for weeks. There was a program that had been doing pop-up antibody testing sites at random in grocery store parking lots. The state wanted to test a sample of 10,000 New York residents to determine what percentage of the population may have already been infected at some point and carried immunity. These testing times and locations were not advertised because they did not want sick people flocking to these sites. A few friends in LTC and I were in agreement to let each other know if we heard anything about one popping up nearby, but we were never able to track down one of these events.

Both of my parents had been in regular contact with me during the rapidly changing time of the outbreak in my facility. The areas where they lived were not nearly as affected as New York at the time. My father was especially interested in the antibody tests and could not wait until I had the test to determine if I'd had a mostly asymptomatic case. So, I had to get tested to make him happy about passing on his rugged genes. I scheduled a test after a coworker started spreading the word that these tests were finally available to the public. To schedule an appointment, I had to answer a series of exposure-related questions on the lab's website. The site very clearly explained that they did not want sick people coming into their business. They only tested for antibodies in asymptomatic people and not for the illness itself. I felt that my coworkers and I were in a gray area. We were most likely exposed regularly, but there was no way to know for sure with our workplace still avoiding resident testing as much as possible.

At the lab, I was brought back immediately and was surprised when the tech started strapping a rubber band around my arm. I had expected a finger-stick and was trying not to fidget while my vein was being tapped for what felt like minutes before determining it was adequate for a blood draw. She was an okay tech, but I can't say it was one of those smooth draws where you barely feel it. I definitely sweated as the needle jerked around in my vein a bit while the tube was screwed on for collection. I had my results by the next morning. I noticed the email had come through as I pulled into my parking space at work. I felt the same nervous anticipation as if I were waiting for a college acceptance letter. Positive! I never thought I'd be so happy to receive a positive result on a medical test.

This occurred on a Friday, and we had to have a focused discussion about the testing because it was to officially start the following week. The facility had been trying desperately to find a lab to accept our test results but had not heard back from any of them at that point. I asked Chad in front of the group if the antibody test results would waive the testing requirement. As I sat next to Pam, I felt like a kid asking the parent you know will give you the answer you want to hear. He confirmed that a positive antibody test would waive the requirement if the test were an actual blood draw and not from a finger-stick. I said that I was good then, and he asked how I pulled that off. I mentioned my loss of taste weeks before. He seemed genuinely happy for me and playfully teased, "You cheated."

The majority of staff then rushed out to labs offering the antibody testing. Everyone was walking around with bruises on their arms for a week after this meeting. Among those who tested positive were at least one of the activities aides, the HR lady, and two out of three of the unit managers. One of these unit managers was pregnant and had been especially careful during this time. She had been granted exemption from high-risk tasks. More surprising than the positives were certain staff who tested negative. Everybody in the building was highly exposed. But certain people had more face to face contact than others. The social worker was constantly in and out of rooms on all units, and the one unit manager who tested negative had been providing a lot of hands-on care during staffing shortages. Everybody wanted that positive antibody result. We were the lucky ones. I was able to sleep well that weekend. This celebratory period was short-lived, however. Pam received an email at eleven p.m. the following Tuesday night with revisions to the original testing requirements. Everybody had to be tested regardless of whether they had been previously diagnosed with a case or tested positive for the antibodies. This was due to the fact that it is unknown how long these antibodies confer immunity, if at all.

I moved onto loophole number two. The facility was still struggling to find a lab willing to process our tests, so most people were getting their testing at the college campus site. Sue and Karen informed me at morning report that there was a pharmacy site which was so much better. You self-administered the test with a Q-tip, which you didn't have to insert into your nostril very far at all. Since the mandate change occurred in the middle of the week, I figured I was still accountable for one test. I scheduled one at the pharmacy for Friday afternoon.

This option could not have been any more convenient or low stress. There was a line of tents set up on one side of the parking lot. You drove up to the first tent and, with windows up, pressed your ID against the window so the employee could get you set up. You were then directed to the next available tent. The tech was initially standing toward the back of the tent, so you could have your window down. They gave instructions on how to administer the test. They were as follows: Remove the Q-tip from the wrapper. Insert into the first nostril (not very far) and swirl around twice. Hold for fifteen seconds. Repeat on the other side. Insert the stick swab end first into the vial. This was the trickiest part—you had to bust off the end of the stick so that the cap could be fastened onto the vial. Sometimes you had to work it a little. The staff was available if you had any questions, but it did not feel like a high-pressure environment. The college girls in belly shirts and tank tops gave the test site a more casual vibe than at the actual college campus site where National Guard soldiers were walking around in fatigues.

I was comfortable with the idea of driving to the pharmacy for the biweekly tests. The following week, the facility found a lab or labs to process our results. We still had the option to get the tests done at other sites, but there was no guarantee that the facility would pay for it. I was never charged by the pharmacy, but would have been willing to pay to not have the nasopharyngeal swab. This was a short week for some staff because of Memorial Day. It took about three days to receive your test results and then another twenty-four hours following your results before your account reset in order to schedule another test. This did not leave enough time to schedule both tests at the pharmacy. I hoped that my company would allow me to telework on Friday in order to be considered a part-time employee for the week. Anybody working twenty-four hours or less per week on site only needed one test for the week. Due to employees taking advantage of this perk in the past, my company required written permission from the administrator to telework. He was out on holiday leave, so this option was out.

Figuring out the onsite testing availability the first week was very frustrating. On Wednesday, Karen and Chad decided that they needed to have a private meeting about it after morning report. The next day Sue and I asked about it and received no direct answer. We had basic questions like where to go, how to sign up, what times were available, who would be conducting the tests, etc. I still did not have these answers when I walked in Friday morning and knew that I would be out of compliance if I did not get swabbed that day. I went straight to Pam's office, and she let me know that the next workshop would be from eleven to one in the beauty shop (which had been unused for months). This was the first day they gave some concrete information about it in morning report.

I wasn't sure who would be behind the closed door when I went for the first test at work. My coworkers had been passing around information about who was the gentlest and who would not push the swab back so far. The housekeeper who had gone into the room for the test before me came out crying, so this didn't help my nerves. It was my favorite nurse, Jill! She said that she wouldn't go in far because she didn't feel right about it given that I had tested positive for the antibodies. She ended up letting me self-administer the test. This was not a laziness or shirking of responsibility on the part of the "corrupt" nurses (and there were several of them). They were simply not comfortable performing a medical procedure on their coworkers. It changed the entire dynamic. So, if there was a way they could justify going a little easier on their colleagues during the test, they would do it. I asked her how far up the nose we were supposed to insert the swab. She pointed to an indent that seemed very far down. I challenged myself and tried to see how far I could insert it myself and made it maybe about a third of the way down. I decided that I would do one in-house test per week and the other at the pharmacy. I knew there was the risk that the nurse I was comfortable with performing my test could call out sick or be on vacation on my test day or be stuck on the unit.

Toward the end of the third week of the biweekly testing requirement, Mark pointed out that I should maybe have the real test at least once for the experience and also for the purpose of solidarity with my coworkers. I felt the same way and knew that day would come, but I wasn't exactly seeking out that experience. The day I was scheduled to have my second test in-house, the HR lady approached me during morning report and said that my test results from the previous week came back inconclusive. I let her know that I had another negative result from the pharmacy that I needed to print for her as well as a planned test that day. She said that should be sufficient. I later learned that a staff member had been kicked out of the building for an inconclusive result. I figured it was because the test was not performed in the torturous manner intended. My office mate also had a "corrupt" nurse but her results had come back negative.

When I went for my test that afternoon there were a handful of people waiting. It was my favorite nurse, as before, but she had been sitting next to me during morning report when HR discussed my inconclusive result. I was first in line and she asked the others to step outside the room. I closed the door and sat down in the salon chair. I wasn't sure if it was standard procedure to ensure privacy for each test or if we were going to continue the same arrangement as the week before. But there was some unspoken communication that we would not be getting away with any more shenanigans moving forward. I tilted my chin up a little and she gently held the back of my head while inserting the swab with a slight twisting motion. What made me most comfortable with Jill is that she has a competent, gentle vibe which makes you more willing to comply. There are several patients who will refuse to participate in treatments or care by other staff but will be more willing when she is present. Probably for this reason, and to her frustration, a disproportionate number of the very difficult psych cases end up on her unit.

I had always assumed that the test would be so traumatic that I would be paralyzed for the duration of it. But I was able to express one word of surprise. I believe it was a "damn" or "whoa." She said, "I know. Pam says we have to go the full depth or else the tests come back inconclusive." She quietly finished counting to thirty and it was over. She was apologetic and I said something about it being about time for me to stop being a bitch about it anyway. My right eye was tearing up, but it was not a painful process, just uncomfortable. Maybe a little burning. I knew she felt bad, so I made sure to tell her she was the best on the way out. I was relieved to have the experience of the full nasopharyngeal swab. It was not as terrible as I had expected, but I still didn't want to go through it biweekly indefinitely.

Some staff were getting headaches and facial swelling, probably due to sinus inflammation during this time. The biweekly testing happened to coincide with spring allergy season, so for those with inflammation already present, it was probably a lot more uncomfortable.

I continued to get nervous about the tests, but since it was happening so often it became routine. A couple weeks in I noticed the staff member in line in front of me was standing up during her test. I asked Jill which position was easier for her, and she said that it actually seems easier for both herself and the one being tested to be standing and facing forward. No craning your neck upward. So, I switched to standing and it is a lot better. I even decided to spice things up one day and request testing in the other nostril. I have a slightly crooked nose and wanted to see if one side would be worse than the other. The left side definitely burned more.

We were able to start once-weekly testing the second week of June. Facilities in parts of the state still in phase one had to continue the twice-weekly testing. I chat with my grandmother daily on my drive home from work. She had become accustomed to my bi-weekly testing and I had transferred my initial anxiety surrounding the procedure onto her. She asked almost daily if I had had my test that day and if the "nice nurse" was there. My testing day became Fridays, and I made sure to let Jill know that when the day came for her to take a three-day weekend, an older woman living in Vermont would have a meltdown.

You can get used to anything. I got so used to the testing that without the constant stress of it in the back of my mind, I completely forgot to show up for my usual testing workshop one day. There were fewer opportunities for in-house testing by this point. Basically, if I didn't remember to go to the workshop on Tuesdays from eleven to one then I had to track down one of the few nurses who perform the tests outside of workshop times. Some staff do this regularly, but I felt bad about it because they are busy and often shorthanded. The pharmacy site in the area was no longer doing the tests. I'm assuming it was because the rest of the country had broken out with the disease and resources were being allocated elsewhere. On this particular day, Sue had a meltdown in between the morning care conferences and I was a little distracted by that. To my surprise, she recovered quickly and actually remembered to get her test that afternoon. I ate lunch, went for my walk, casually worked on some billing books, and then realized I had forgotten to go in for testing before the afternoon round of meetings. It was 1:25 when I looked at the clock. Jill was out grabbing lunch before the next set of meetings.

I had a couple of care conferences with Jill that afternoon and hoped that I could get her to test me afterward. She had purchased a scratch-off lottery ticket on her lunch break. It was a very confusing poker game which teases you with parts that look like winning hands, but aren't. There were a few minutes during which we thought she might have become a millionaire. I didn't feel right about bothering her for the test after learning that she was not. To be honest, I was pretty bummed out by the disappointment too. I wandered around looking for another nurse. I called my second choice. No luck. I went to the HR lady to out myself and see if she could help me troubleshoot. She mentioned that there were a few others who needed testing on that day. Before I could find out the details on when these others would be tested and by whom, a flood of people came into the office and stormed it from the hallway as well. I had been a brief interruption during her handling of some unknown crisis. I retreated back to my office.

The next morning Chad gave a reminder that anyone who was not in compliance with the testing regulation would be escorted out of the building. I wondered at what point they would know who was not in compliance. Would I actually be escorted out and by whom? I felt that anything short of someone literally taking me by the arm and walking me out would have been a huge disappointment. I didn't want to be disappointed, so I continued to seek out other options. I had my second-choice testing nurse, Mitch, in care conferences that day. He was the first-choice tester for people who were afraid of the test because he did not swab as deep as required.

It turned out that there were a few other reliable staff who were also out of compliance on that day. Interestingly, as I walked over to Mitch's office for my test, Jill happened to be going over to that unit. I got to the office first and Mitch directed me around the corner so "people won't see how half-assed I do this." Right before he administered the test, Jill walked in. He was like, "Jill, what brings you over to this unit?" She had to come into the office to use the copier and the timing could not have been more hilarious. I could tell he was uncomfortable trying to administer the test in his style in front of a nurse who does it properly. It is a lot more comfortable getting it done half-assed. But . . . loyalty. I will continue to visit Jill on Tuesdays until what feels like forever right now.

Chapter 10: The Asymptomatics

Around the time that staff were required to start bi-weekly testing, there was also pressure from the outside to test all residents in the building. They would not be undergoing regular testing, but they needed to do a sweep of the entire building. Chad pushed this off for as long as he could saying that he did not feel it was necessary because we were at the tail end of the outbreak and that it would only create mass panic among the residents' families. Unlike the staff, the residents did have a choice in the matter. I was surprised by how many agreed to the testing. There were only three in the building who would not consent to the test. The resident testing was performed by the same nurses who did the staff testing. They were the only ones in the building who had been offered fit testing for N95 respirators.

The results came in three batches and were shocking. The first batch of results came in the morning of Thursday, May 21st. There were nine positives (36-43). One was a repeat positive, which was an oversight; they did not want to test those who had already been counted. The positives were mostly asymptomatic. The second batch of results came in later that day. There were nine more positives (44-52). Friday morning, we received the results for the remaining residents. There were seven more positives (53-59). For some reason, there was one more positive result from the health department over the weekend (60).

There was a total of twenty-six positive results from a sweep of the building, which occurred almost two months after the initial outbreak and when things seemed resolved. We were no longer following dozens of people for fevers and respiratory symptoms on line lists. When someone tested positive for the virus, they were put on contact precautions for two weeks. This entailed keeping the resident restricted to their room and using the N95 respirators. Positive residents could be roomed with other positive residents; in healthcare this practice is called cohorting. This made me realize that the majority of residents had probably already had the illness and these were just the ones who hadn't cleared the virus yet. Chad was smart to put off this testing for as long as he could in order to be able to report a smaller number to the Department of Health. In actuality, it was unlikely there were many residents who had *not* had the illness at some point already. The most vulnerable ones had already died or been obviously symptomatic. The lucky ones had, like the majority of the positives in this building sweep, probably been asymptomatic carriers sometime within the previous two months.

The high number of positive cases added a lot more work in that the families had the right to be contacted daily with updates on their loved ones' condition. This had Chad all riled up. He said that it was communism to require staff to update the family daily. And he thought it was even more over-the-top that the requirement also specified that staff use the family's communication method of choice. I'm assuming the communication methods were phone call or email. I did not find this unreasonable at all considering the illness kills a high percentage of cases in this population and the family was not allowed to visit. But I could always rely on Chad to provide good quotes plucked directly from some ultra-conservative radio show on his morning commute.

Now that we were forced to officially recognize the positive cases, they needed to be quarantined. The cases were spread out pretty much evenly throughout the building. There was some discussion about which unit should be used to contain these residents. It made the most sense to me to use the rehab unit, which had been used as the high-risk area all along. The dialysis residents had already been moved there as part of the planning process and had all tested positive by this point. All new admits start on that unit and are observed carefully for fourteen days before moving them to one of the other units. The state was not allowing the facility to take new residents at this time. Two out of three unit managers had tested positive for antibodies, indicating that they had already been exposed to the illness.

For whatever reason, the unit chosen was run by the unit manager who had not tested positive for the illness or antibodies yet. This was Jill's unit. She was an LPN filling in temporarily as unit manager until the facility could find an RN to take over the position. Everyone had concerns about the implications COVID-19 could have on themselves or their families. There were pregnancies, children at home, health concerns, older family members, etc. Jill had a special needs son living at home with severe asthma. During the summer there had been at least two instances when he had to go to the emergency room. Something as commonplace as high humidity was enough to bring on serious breathing difficulty for this boy. If COVID-19 were brought into this household, his life would be in serious danger. This was never considered by the powers that be. And even though the staff on this unit were running a dedicated COVID-19 wing, there was never any talk of hazard pay.

That Friday afternoon, after we received the final test results, the entire place was turned upside down with room changes. It was a complete clusterfuck. There was nobody really in charge of the event, so Amanda had this dropped on her. The activities department had a lot dropped on them during this time. The dining room filled up with beds as the moves continued. I left my office periodically to see if there was any way to be useful. Every time I did my rounds, it seemed like there were groups of people standing around like high school cliques. Nobody had any information about what was going on or what would be happening next. I bugged Amanda a couple times for assignments but felt like more of a nuisance than a help.

At one point, I ended up in a room with one of our dialysis residents. The unit manager and I were packing his clothing and belongings from his closet into plastic bags. I felt invasive because the man and his roommate were both eating their lunches at the time. I apologized for disrupting, but neither really seemed to take much notice of our presence.

A man in the room across the hallway (35) was not so resigned to the situation. The yelling could be heard throughout the entire unit and probably beyond. He had reached his breaking point with the constant changes. He had recently been refused treatment by his dialysis center due to exposure. He was required to get testing before going back. He tested positive two days before we received the test results for everyone else in the building. He had to go to a different dialysis clinic at a different time until he tested negative for the illness. He had also been forced to move to the rehab unit when all the dialysis patients were moved there. Now he was being told he had to move again, and he was not having it!

He was asymptomatic during this time. But three months after his initial COVID-19 diagnosis, he started feeling sick to his stomach. He began vomiting and spiked a fever. The next day, he had trouble getting comfortable because of various aches and pains in his back, neck, and torso. He started vomiting again and his fever increased. He had severe abdominal pains. He was sent to the ER and the hospital admitted him due to abnormal labs. He tested positive for COVID-19 and passed away within two days. This came as a shock to everyone because he was very young. Aside from very high blood sugars, he was doing pretty well. He was working toward discharging and moving to Florida to live with his aunt.

Back to the mass move . . .. The staff's use of PPE that afternoon seemed to be left to individual discretion. There was an activities aide wearing a face shield, and I wondered where she had gotten ahold of one since I hadn't seen them used in our building before. I think this employee was one of the drivers. Many people enjoyed the opportunity to dress more casually. We got "hero" T-shirts that morning and most were wearing these with jeans. I felt the general consensus was that we had all obviously been extensively exposed by that point and were not overly stressed about it. This was a long, confusing day, and some residents had clothing and other items go missing among the chaos.

One of the few residents who had refused the in-house COVID-19 testing (61) had a series of mini strokes a couple of weeks later. She went to the hospital and tested positive. COVID-19 puts people at an increased risk for blood clots. D-dimer is a protein fragment which can be detected in blood when a clot begins to break down. This lab test is used to help determine if someone may have a clot. Nursing had observed that some of our COVID-19 positive patients had very elevated d-dimer lab values. This is not a lab I was familiar with prior to the outbreak. This woman recovered and returned to the facility.

Less than two weeks after the building sweep, we were already accepting new admissions. There was some discussion about whether or not to retest the residents on the COVID unit. The administrator initially did not want to out of fear that we would still have positives, but Mitch pointed out that we should in order to cover ourselves in case the virus started to spread again. They waited a little longer to be sure that everyone would have cleared the virus. Only one of the dialysis residents (38) still came back positive. I think he tested positive again a week after that. It took several tries for him to get a negative test result.

Before we had even begun the discussion about retesting the residents, Chad grumbled about how one of our sister facilities had received recognition for being the first in the company to be COVID-free after an outbreak. He felt that we had already achieved that status. I quickly learned that he and higher-ups in corporate were using the terms "asymptomatic" and "COVID-free" interchangeably. These words are not interchangeable! COVID-free implies that the disease is not present. An asymptomatic carrier has the illness and does not have any symptoms. They can still infect other people. Some research has even suggested that asymptomatic carriers can be more infectious than symptomatic carriers. Yet it is these people with little to no understanding of the science who have the autonomy to make the important decisions about how to handle the pandemic.

CHAPTER 11: THE SLOW PHASE

There was a period of time when the number of patients was so low there wasn't a lot of work. The facility can hold close to 130 residents at full capacity, and we usually had very few empty beds. For a time, we were not allowed to bring in new admissions or even take back our own residents who were ready to return from hospitals. I do not know the specific period of time or parameters we had to meet in order to open back up. What I do know is that this was not a decision made by the company. It was imposed from The Department of Health, most likely because we had reached outbreak status. More accurately, it was now known that we had reached outbreak status. This is why the administrator was hesitant about retesting the residents. At our lowest point, the census was in the seventies.

I started rationing my documentation so I would have some actual work to do daily. I described my feelings during this time to a friend undergoing the same situation in this way: "COVID is doing weird things psychologically to people. Right now, I have no desire to work this job, and I don't think I'm normally a lazy person. It's kind of like a depressed feeling from having no impact (which I feel to a lesser extent in LTC anyway), but it's a lot worse since there are so few residents and it's more complicated to meet with them." She felt that this accurately described her current state also.

Mark and I decided to take a staycation, because it became clear at this point in the year that unnecessary travel was not in anyone's best interest. But that did not mean that we would let our vacation time go to waste. Not after going through a COVID-19 outbreak in my workplace! We live in an area where several healthcare facilities had been hit with the virus. Mark was also dealing with the effects of the virus behind the scenes. The employees in his office had started teleworking in March. Since New York City was the epicenter of the virus in the United States, there were several deaths of healthcare workers that needed investigation. The city office could not handle the volume of investigations on their own, so other offices in the region were picking up these cases.

One day we decided to go for a drive to explore some of the rural towns in the area. The restaurants had just opened back up with strict rules in place. We found a little diner and went inside for breakfast. Like most business places, there was a sign clearly stating that masks must be worn inside by customers when not seated at the table. There were a few other parties seated and having their meals. It was obvious on this late weekday morning that the others were locals. The one waitress/owner was casually chatting with some of the customers. We noticed a man who appeared to be in his fifties get up and say goodbye to the waitress as he walked out without a mask. He had two young girls with him and was not enforcing that they wear masks either. We did not see this party enter the restaurant, so we were unsure if they had worn masks in and then didn't bother to put them back on before walking out or if they didn't bother to follow the rules at all.

As soon as the door closed behind them, the waitress discussed her frustration with a couple of tables of women. She felt that it was important to follow the rules put in place by the experts but found it awkward to be put in the position of enforcing them in her own business. She was offended that people ignored instructions clearly marked on a sign on the front door. However, she didn't want to lose business by getting into an argument over something that had become highly politicized.

It was an odd feeling to be so immersed in the illness daily at work and yet the majority of people in the community did not know anyone who had been affected by it. One of the ladies started talking about how she had been reading about how masks may actually be harmful to your health. It's not healthy to be restricted of oxygen like that . . . bacteria can get trapped around your airways . . . This is the type of scene that healthcare workers and actually anyone with critical thinking skills is frustrated by fairly often. I just wanted to say, "Freshen up your coffee, ladies, because I've got some stories for you." But during a time when science is often ignored, this could have been more annoyance than I wanted to deal with on my vacation week.

CHAPTER 12: STAFFING

While there was inconsistent notification about our residents who tested positive, there was never any mention of our coworkers who went out on quarantine. It was unclear how many people we had out sick at any given time. A news article that came out shared that fifteen staff members had tested positive at that point in time. This was before the mandatory staff testing was implemented. Therefore, these staff most likely felt ill enough to seek out testing on their own. I had only been aware of 4 cases from a previous news article and only knew the identity of one. This was a dietary aide who rarely left the kitchen and presumably caught the virus from contaminated dishes. I was shocked to learn from the news that my workplace was now up to 15 confirmed staff cases.

There was some talk of people choosing to stay home because they could make more money on unemployment with the federal supplement than they would working full-time. I don't think this really affected my workplace, as nobody was laid off. The facility was not really in a position to fire people either. I did not hear any stories of staff "acting up" in order to be fired to try to get the unemployment benefit. Theoretically, the staff in the riskiest positions have low enough salaries that they would have made more if there was an easy way to choose this option. I think that illness and perhaps childcare issues were the main reasons for staff shortages. Based on the antibody test results, most staff who contracted the illness were probably asymptomatic and did not even get their two weeks off to quarantine.

The secretary from the rehab unit, the one who was disturbed by families sneaking open window visits, had temporarily moved her workstation to the social work office when the second social worker bailed. I had heard that she was out on quarantine. The disturbing thing was that even people who had close contact with positive staff members were kept in the dark. You had to rely on the integrity of the sick person who could decide if they were willing to notify their close contacts or not. She had informed Sue that she was out with the virus because they shared the office. I had a similar situation when one of my office mates was out sick for an entire week with pending test results.

One afternoon shortly after the secretary returned, I went into the office to fix myself a coffee. I'm very curious about people's health situations, nosey even, but she is a very kind woman and was open to sharing her story. Her fear that she would bring the virus home to her aging mother came true. Fortunately, her mother had a milder case than her own. She had a high fever and chills that lasted for several days. One of the most interesting effects from the virus was that she no longer craved cigarettes after recovering. This was not a conscious decision to improve her health after having a scare. The desire was no longer there.

Before this conversation, I never knew how involved the contact-tracing program was in our area. It was amazing. She would receive a phone call daily and had to go to her window and wave to a contact tracer who would physically show up at her residence to confirm her presence. She also said that food packages were delivered a couple times when she and her mother got low on supplies. These were a surprise. Quarantined individuals did not have the option to be high maintenance and put in a food order. They would receive a package that could contain a cut of meat, beans, etc. A few months after hearing her story, I was in my car checking my messages before leaving for the day. I saw the secretary drive by with a cigarette in her hand. I thought I should mention that so as not to mislead readers into thinking COVID-19 might be a miracle cure for smokers.

The number of residents who tested positive during the building-wide testing surprised us all. Since the staff-testing mandate started around the same time, there were also some surprise asymptomatic staff cases. Our director of therapy almost lost her mind with a sudden two-week quarantine. She would have enjoyed it had she been able to purchase gardening supplies beforehand. But the staff testing started well past the main outbreak, so those who tested positive were a little blindsided by it.

An activities aide tested positive, which was surprising because she had tested positive for the antibodies. Most likely her case had not fully resolved yet, but her body had begun building up a defense. The activities aides made up the bulk of the non-direct care staff who had to step in and serve as aides when we reached critical staffing shortages. When this girl had fulfilled her two-week quarantine and was planning her return to work with her director, they decided to have her come in one afternoon. She was told that she would have to wait until the next morning in order to get another swab to confirm that she was now negative. However, they were willing to allow her to come in that afternoon/evening if she was willing to serve as a nursing aide.

There were always news stories in the New York area about healthcare workers dying from the illness. Mark was investigating five of those deaths for his work. It made me realize how lucky my facility had been so far that no staff had been killed by the virus yet. The first medical professional to die from the virus who I had worked with personally was a doctor who covered several facilities in the area. He was found dead in his hotel room after recovering from a month-long battle with the virus. It was suspected that a blood clot had formed during his illness and led to a stroke.

Another was a nurse who I had worked with at both Arbor Park and Falls View. He was a very nice man and also a reliable nurse. I found out that he had passed away from a lung disease. The details were very sparse. He had a collapsed lung. I was sad to hear the news of his passing and felt that an unspecified lung disease was very suspect during this time. He appeared to be fairly young and healthy.

We have had some massive staff turnover since my start at Dutch Meadows. This is not unusual in a long-term care setting and is not due to the pandemic. In the nursing department, I work most closely with the unit managers, so I am most affected by the quality of the person in this position. Our rehab unit has had four in fewer than eight months. The first one was the best at the job in my opinion. She was scattered, but I appreciated that she advocated for me when I was repeatedly skipped over during morning report when I first started the job. She had some kind of altercation with Karen and left on the spot.

The next one was an older woman with a mysterious background. She would work her way around basic small talk questions like where she worked prior to taking the job. Mitch was the assistant manager on the unit at the time and felt that he had to babysit her because she would try leaving for the day before the work had been completed. She was fired for taking off before the DOH left during an infection control survey. The next one seemed promising the first week or two. Then she sat in the office Facetiming with family and followed up on things about 20 percent of the time. She lasted a few months. The most recent one seemed very assertive. She was there for about a week.

The unit currently has no leadership. Generally, when a unit has no manager, it is the responsibility of upper level nursing to fill the role temporarily, whether it be for a sick day or longer while searching for new candidates. The coverage could be provided by the ADON or DON. Mitch has since been promoted to some vague position. None of these upper level nurses even check up on these units throughout the day.

The shortest term of employment for a unit manager was about one hour. She came in and was filling out the paperwork in the HR office. She completed the paperwork and was to join us in morning report for introductions. She had excused herself from the HR office to grab her water bottle out of her car before the start of the meeting. The HR lady came into morning report to tell us that she thought she had bailed. We thought she was joking or that maybe the new nurse forgot the punch-in code to get back inside the building, but nope. She climbed into her car and took off. She probably heard someone coughing on the unit and was like, well, f— that! She may have dodged a bullet, because that was during the period of time when the virus was spreading at the quickest rate. Her hour-long "employment" in our building should have been considered an exposure.

After everyone at the facility had pretty much recovered from the virus, we had a lot of very low-quality agency staff coming into the building. Among them was a man who arrived from the city with a cat. He did not have time to drop the cat off at the hotel because he was brought straight to the facility to report to work. Having a pet in the building had been banned since the onset of the pandemic, but an exception was made in order to get staff in the building. The cat was initially allowed to roam the conference room until it urinated on the floor. It was then contained in the HR office. The cat came to the building twice.

I was scanning through the progress notes for a resident during morning report and noticed that there were a few notes for treatments stating "didn't get to it" or "focused on med pass." I found this bizarre and leaned over to Jill, who was sitting next to me and said, "Can you do that?" She was appalled and brought this up with Karen. No, you cannot document your weak excuses for not providing prescribed treatments in someone's medical record.

We also had a lady show up who spent a lot of time sitting on the unit with her feet up. Usually she would do this visibly right in the hallway. One time, however, an activities aide almost had a heart attack when she went into the dayroom to fetch something for a resident and switched on the light to discover this woman had been sitting in the dark in the corner of the room playing on her phone. Another woman from the agency was kicked out immediately when she was reported to have been mocking one of the residents.

Toward the end of the outbreak in the facility, one doctor began to unravel like a schizophrenic off his medication. His hygiene was lacking, and he smelled of body odor. He was very arrogant in general and therefore didn't receive much sympathy. He would make himself comfortable in the unit managers' office with his feet up on their desks. I limited my interaction with this doctor because he had been fired from Falls View while I was working there and I did not trust his intentions, especially after the coercing of residents to change their code statuses.

He did not last long at this place either. His arrogance and poor hygiene were the least of his concerning behaviors. He was ordering unnecessary medical tests on the residents to further his research.

He requested repeat antibody tests, which would have provided no benefit for the individual. Getting approval for a research study takes a lot of time and requires Institutional Review Board (IRB) approval if you're receiving federal funding. This is a group formally designated to approve or disapprove studies involving human subjects based on ethical considerations. There are even stricter guidelines when you're working with a vulnerable population—many of our residents would have not even had the capacity to consent. So, he was given an exit date and let the paperwork pile up since he was no longer invested in the place. And it took many months to get him out, so there was a long period of time when we didn't know if he was or wasn't serving as the MD for the building. He would show up sporadically.

While the MDs only show up a couple times a week at a facility, the nurse practitioners (NPs) are supposed to be there as a full-time *doctor*. We didn't have the best situation in this department either. There was a young man who had just become a NP after previously working as a RN. It seemed to have gone to his head. He had a huge sense of entitlement. One day I was working with the wound round team and he strolled by and dropped something into the trash bag hanging off the side of the nurse's med cart. She was like, "Did you just put chewing tobacco in there?" Sure enough, there was a little clump of loose-leaf tobacco in there that he had been chewing while on the job. His workdays got shorter and shorter. He wanted to make his morning tee times. He had accepted a job at another facility but put off his start date there due to the difficulty of finding a new NP to replace him during COVID-19. Since he was such a hero for choosing to stay longer, he must have felt justified in shortening his days even further. I usually come in for work around eight thirty a.m., and he would typically be on his way out when I arrived. He unfortunately was the one to train the new guy. So, the new guy also seemed to think that a few hours in the building was sufficient to collect a full-time salary.

These guys are not, however, the worst-case scenario of NPs. The worst NP I worked with also happened to be the best. She was great at her job. I was able to pull a lot of valuable information from her detailed documentation. She would also pull information from other departments and give credit appropriately. I would be flattered when she would put a quote from one of my assessments in a progress note. Here's the catch: she had a drug problem. There were times when she would be stumbling all over herself. She wore a lot of makeup and occasionally she would have lipstick applied around her mouth about an inch from her lips. It was hard to bust her for the drug problem because she had legitimate health issues and some of the drugs may have been prescribed. But it was obvious that the medication wasn't being taken correctly.

The problem had been addressed with the medical director on more than one occasion. He reassured the administrator that her medications had the side effect of drowsiness. I wondered at what point it would be considered inappropriate to allow her to practice medicine. At least one family member pulled a resident out against medical advice because they were so disgusted with the situation. She ended up leaving the facility in handcuffs for a prescription-related crime. I found out later that she had crashed her car into the building the week before. One of my coworkers had worked with her previously in a hospital and he said that she did the same thing and was fired from that job. People like this are probably having no trouble at all finding jobs during COVID-19. If they didn't before, they sure won't now.

CHAPTER 13: SISTER FACILITIES

The company that runs Dutch Meadows owns many other facilities across the state. So, when one facility is mandated by the state to halt admissions and readmissions, another one of the facilities can pick up these patients to minimize profit losses. You would assume that facilities within the same company would be working together, but this does not appear to be the case. There have been many times in which a problem employee from one site would be fired and picked up by another as if there was no communication whatsoever between the facilities. The shuffling around of patients and competition between these facilities does create some tension at times.

Venice, one of our sister facilities, is only about an hour and a half west. We lost a female resident to that place because she apparently loved the coffee so much that she was not interested in returning when we could take back our residents. When a coworker remarked to the Corporate Director of Nutrition that she wished her facility was more like Venice, she was told that Venice's food service operations were not something to aspire to because the facility had one of the highest rates of unintended weight loss. This was in part due to the kitchen using COVID-19 as an excuse to only serve soup and sandwiches for every lunch and dinner. They also made the news when a resident put up a video of herself on social media speaking out about the conditions. Her family got involved and staged a protest outside the building, which caught some news attention. I watched her video and thought that all of her concerns sounded pretty accurate to how things are run at Dutch Meadows and Falls View.

I was surprised that Falls View's outbreak came so much later than our own. But they did have an advantage in terms of the actual setup of the building, which is spread out over six floors. Only staff could take the stairs and there was a punch code to access the stairwells. The elevators were accessible to residents on floors two through six. Residents rarely visited other floors, though. They would generally travel between their own floor and the second floor, which contained most of the public spaces and administrative offices.

They were also taking whatever measures they could to prevent the spread of infection. They started limiting the number of staff in morning report to make social distancing easier. Only one person per department was needed to represent and masks were nonnegotiable. There was a scare at the end of March when the administrator tested positive. This was a scare not only for Falls View but also for other facilities within the company. Supposedly the administrator had attended a social gathering with a group of other admins the weekend before developing a fever and testing positive. But no further infections developed for almost a month.

Once the first resident infection was discovered, things progressed very quickly. I do not believe that the infection spread any more quickly in this facility. More likely, their quick action revealed the extent of the problem that Dutch Meadows had chosen to pretend wasn't happening. A resident was sent out from the locked dementia unit after a seizure. She tested positive in the hospital. Upon hearing this news, the facility immediately tested six residents on that unit and all tested positive. Then some residents on Unit Two started developing symptoms.

Then someone tested positive on the third floor. It was interesting that the sixth floor was not among the first with positive cases. This was the originally chosen "staging area" where all dialysis patients and new admits were monitored. There was a story going around that one of the nursing staff had tested positive the first week in April and continued to work without notifying anyone at the facility. The administrator had caught wind of this rumor and was talking of firing the staff member once their identity was discovered. This type of behavior would not have been something that could have gone unnoticed in the county where Dutch Meadows is located because of the strict contact-tracing program.

However, like most of my information on Falls View during the pandemic, it was received third person through friends still working in the building. This rumor about the positive staff member contrasted with a news article that came out later with data from a study by the New York State Department of Health. The state confirmed that Falls View was one of half a dozen facilities in which a COVID-19 outbreak was initiated by taking in COVID-19 positive residents from the hospital. But many were hesitant to trust this report as they felt it is an attempt by the state to cover up a reckless decision to require nursing homes to accept COVID-19 positive patients This feeling was reinforced by the fact that the report initially claimed that fifty-eight facilities had outbreaks originating from this mandate and then later changed that number to only six.

One positive change came about quickly as a result of the outbreak. Falls View had a smoking program for residents. The administrator had previously tried to do away with the program and received a lot of pushback from staff, mainly from the nurses who smoked and empathized with the residents. When the topic of ending the program was initially broached, many felt that it was a violation of resident rights to not allow them to smoke. I was never on board with that argument, considering that hospitals and other facilities can give nicotine-addicted patients patches while being treated. Why should health insurance pay for people to be treated in a skilled nursing facility where people are allowed to actively damage their bodies? This "service" at Falls View attracted a certain type of client as well. People would discharge from other facilities to Falls View specifically for that purpose. I recall meeting with a malnourished patient who was a picky eater to come up with a plan to help her gain weight. She was agreeable to having a visit with the diet tech in order to make menu adjustments, however, she made it clear that I would need to instruct her to come between the scheduled smoke breaks. She was among many who prioritized their right to smoke well above the quality of their care.

The staff member overseeing the smoke breaks held all of the residents' cigarettes in a cart and was responsible for doling them out and lighting the cigarettes. I believe they were allowed up to two cigarettes per break. Some staff were upset about being exposed to secondhand smoke. During the winter there had been concerns about the smoking program promoting the spread of the flu and norovirus. At times, specific units had to be locked down due to outbreaks of these illnesses, but the smokers still insisted on pushing their way out for their scheduled smoke breaks. This became even more of a concern when COVID-19 arrived, so this program was ended.

Falls View made the news quickly. Pretty much any facility with COVID-19 positive residents makes the news. This was the point at which residents started passing away at a rapid rate. Staffing was terrible as people were out sick. The DON started working overnights. I started worrying about one of the nurses who had health problems and was working part time in the facility during this time. She had such bad asthma that she could sometimes be heard wheezing from across the room. I became close with this nurse while working with her at Arbor Park as part of a small team to help one of our bariatric residents reach her weight loss goals. One time we had discussed premonitions at length, so I felt she would not think I was crazy for reaching out. She no longer works at the facility. This was a relief to me because her life would be in jeopardy if she caught the illness. This is another example of how the company does not take the health status of its workers into consideration. On the one hand, health is a very personal matter. But on the other, it is frustrating that people with obvious health concerns have to take matters into their own hands to seek out accommodations or quit. And I doubt a request for accommodations would be well received.

My former co-RD, Vera, was also struggling emotionally during this time and it was affecting her sleep. It was hard to see my friends at other nursing homes going through the same phases of the outbreak that I had experienced. I wanted to tell them the worst was over once they started becoming stressed, but I also didn't want to lie. Vera is pretty tough, so I would tell her honestly that things would get worse before they got better. My favorite example of her toughness is when she told off a needy maintenance worker when we were swamped with work during a state survey.

He was one of those people who gets comfortable way too quickly. From his first day on the job he would open the door to our office and ask awkward questions like "Are you alone?" and "Are you married?" It was close to impossible for one of the women in the nutrition office to sneak off to the bathroom at the other end of the hallway without some comment. It became a sort of game for the dietitians in the afternoon. Sometimes one of us would almost make it and then hear a creepy drawn-out, "I seeee yoooou." You would then catch a glimpse of him out of the corner of your eye flexing and extending his index finger in your direction. We had concluded that he was probably not dangerous, but he was demanding of our time, which warranted setting boundaries when the workload was high. So, when he cracked open our door when we were in the middle of trying to troubleshoot kitchen problems after already staying late for survey, Vera, without turning to face him, lifted up her hand and said sternly, "We need to focus right now." This interaction bought us some space for at least a week afterward and Vera instantly reached superhero status in my mind.

Falls View really suffered with many staff going out sick at the same time. Basically, the entire administrative suite was out sick with the administrator trying to keep the place together on his own. Due to the staffing crisis, one day they had to send out an entire unit to three other facilities. This was the one unit that had no known positive cases at the time. This was an all-hands-on-deck situation. Morning report was cancelled as every staff member in the building worked together to pack up these residents and send them out. They did get some pushback for this as the gossip made it back to Dutch Meadows that they had not adequately communicated these transfers to the family members of the residents who were shipped out—thirty-five residents in total.

Falls View and Dutch Meadows were comparable in their stinginess to provide any type of hazard pay to their staff. Bigwig corporate guy Jack had promised "hero pay" to all staff at Falls View. Neither facility provided any type of hazard pay to anyone. They did create bonuses for nursing staff, but this was only to ensure adequate staffing and was by no means hazard pay. Nursing staff could receive bonuses for perfect attendance during the two-week pay period. The more highly credentialed the nurse, the higher the bonus. An RN could make an additional $500, an LPN $250, and a CNA $125. These bonuses did not reflect the amount of exposure they had. A CNA who is responsible for direct care, including changing and feeding residents, would be exposed at a much higher rate than the RNs who mainly attend meetings and manage staff. The CNAs make barely above minimum wage. There was a maintenance director at Falls View who had to continue working while undergoing chemotherapy. There had been a fundraising party for him during the winter. His prognosis was bleak, but he could not afford to stop working during this time.

My all-time favorite ongoing Falls View scandal relates to some housing which the facility provides for agency staff who are bussed in from the city. There are a few rundown houses within a short walk of the building that the facility owns. I have always been curious about these places. They really seemed like a liability to me because there was no oversight of them. Occasionally the DON would have to enter one of the buildings to confront employees or a maintenance worker would have to go in to make a repair. One of these repairs involved cleaning feces out of the shower after the toilet had clogged and people started using the bathtub for that purpose. The nutrition office was located next to the maintenance shop, so when I worked there the maintenance workers would occasionally shock us with stories about these places. The maintenance director told me I was welcome to take a peek inside any of these buildings since I was an employee, however, I never got up the nerve to do so. These two departments, along with central supply and housekeeping, were located in the basement, and these employees were lovingly referred to as "basement dwellers."

Gossip made it back to Dutch Meadows that there had been a major incident related to one of these flophouses. The story was shared by Karen during a very relaxed QAPI (quality assurance and performance improvement) meeting, so there was most likely some embellishment. Apparently, all hell broke loose in one of the houses and the DON was called in to intervene. This was the new DON who couldn't have been there longer than a month. The woman walked into a scene straight out of a movie. There were people getting drunk and high ten minutes prior to starting their shifts. There was oral sex openly in progress. Supposedly the young administrator cried and wandered off saying he needed a nap when he got the news. The reason corporate even knew about the drama was because it was not contained within the house. This day included a drug overdose, people falling over coming into work, debauchery in the streets, and brawls on the front porch. At least two people lost their jobs that day.

Around this time, the sibling rivalry really heated up between Dutch Meadows and Falls View. Apparently, Dutch Meadows screwed over Falls View by refusing to take back one of their residents—a very difficult one who had pulled a knife on the SLP while in the hospital. The admissions director at Falls View was livid and expressed her disgust for our facility over the phone to at least one of the local hospitals. We had several of their difficult residents who were referred to as "Falls View Specials" that they refused to take back. Dutch Meadows made it difficult for them to take back the "good" ones that they wanted back. Falls View was requesting a negative COVID-19 test prior to taking back their residents. Dutch Meadows refused to provide it. Eventually Falls View must have relaxed this requirement because I know Dutch Meadows was still refusing to test residents in the facility, but some of Falls View's good residents were returned.

Chapter 14: Filling Up Quickly

When we were cleared to start taking patients back, we started with our previous residents who were ready to return from hospitals or temporarily living in one of our sister facilities. Some residents did not wish to return and many did not survive the outbreak. With enormous pressure to fill the beds, we ended up taking in a lot of residents who were profitable short-term, but were not good long-term investments. Our long Thursday meetings focus on maximizing profit by providing services for those who could benefit and trying to discharge the others as quickly and as safely as possible. Vera and I refer to this meeting as the money-grubber meeting. Nobody likes this meeting, and tensions run high. We ended up with a lot of homeless people, mental health patients, and drug seekers. With these populations it is not easy to plan a safe discharge, so they end up in long-term care. Facilities prefer rehab patients to long-term care because the most profit comes from the rehab department.

One of the most thrilling cases was a man who was well over six feet tall and close to 400 pounds. Right from the start, this man smuggled in two bottles of clonazepam in a cigar box, which he had somehow stashed in his prosthetic leg. I was a little impressed, to be honest, with the storage containers for these pills.

The cigar box had some kind of engraving on it and the bottles inside were clear glass with cork tops. It looked pretty classy, like an old-school medical sales display. We had a care conference with this man the following week and he could really play the game. He was polite, articulate, and expressed his concerns about receiving individualized care as a young person in a facility with so many older folks.

This act did not last long. He pulled a knife on a nurse when she found black tar heroin in his belongings. He called Sue a c***. He threw a fan at Pam. He was not supposed to have a fan anyway, so this was removed. A fan kept mysteriously reappearing in his room and staff suspected that he might have been smuggling in some of his contraband inside of it. He would take silverware off his meal trays and use it to dig the locks out of the window and receive items this way. The kitchen had to start sending plastic utensils for this resident.

It was suspected that he was also sneaking alcohol to a man in an adjoining room, which shared a bathroom. This older man went out to one of his appointments and was sent out to the hospital when he became unresponsive. His lab work came back showing that he was drunk. Karen did not seem to want to admit that this older man was at risk due to living in close proximity to the psychopath. She suggested that he might have auto-brewery syndrome. This is a rare medical condition where the bacteria in your digestive tract ferment carbs and make you drunk without consuming any alcohol. I had never even heard of this syndrome. It is real, but very rare. But she refused to acknowledge that he could have received alcohol while in the facility. So instead, she suggested that he might have a rare medical condition for which he had no diagnosis. Her concern was not great enough to have a doctor look into it. It was just one of the many instances of saying ridiculous crap for attention. He did, however, have a diagnosis for alcoholism. And the smuggler had been looking for this man while he was out. So, it was easy to figure out what happened.

One day, the staff searched the smuggler's room while he was outside working with therapy. They found more contraband, including an emptied-out pen which had been filled with cocaine. This man needed to leave. He was young and completely alert and oriented. He was served a thirty-day notice. We can technically discharge people to a homeless shelter. I was worried about the well-being of the older alcoholic in the meantime. Upon receiving the notice, he assured the staff that he would be staying for a long, long time and that he would be making everyone's life a living hell.

The company brought in one of their lawyers to plan this discharge so that it would not come back on us later. It was decided that the facility needed to offer him a hotel room to discharge to as an alternative to the homeless shelter. This option did not make sense to me, but I'm not a lawyer. On the drive there, he let the staff know that he would be checking out of the hotel, pocketing the money, and staying with his son. Very soon after his discharge, the facility was contacted with news that he wanted to return to us from the hospital.

Apparently, his son wanted nothing to do with him. We were curious about why he had been admitted to the hospital. We assumed a drug overdose, but admissions did not want to ask questions in case they interpreted any inquiries as interest.

Like the drug dealer, the next patient was also very young. He came into the facility to recover after surviving his second shooting. He started telling staff conflicting stories about everything from his housing to his marital status to his involvement in the shooting. In one of the Thursday meetings, someone proposed that he was most likely telling conflicting stories because he wanted to avoid discharge where the gang responsible for his injuries could finish the job since he survived. This turned into a heated debate with an even split of staff who felt that he was a threat to the facility and those who thought that the gang would wait until his discharge to try anything. I hoped the latter were right, because the facility is one story with windows in every room. It's not the most secure location from a gun violence perspective. Probably more concerning to the company was the fact that he had to go out to the hospital for a couple days and tested positive for COVID-19 (64).

These places will also take patients whom they cannot accommodate. Vegetarians are tricky. We do not have a dedicated vegetarian menu, which is annoying because it is not an uncommon request. It is considered a food preference, so we need to manually go in and switch out all items with meat for something else. And we have very limited options. We are lucky if they are pescatarian because then we can add fish entrees and tuna fish sandwiches to the very limited protein options. They will usually receive veggie burgers, egg salad, peanut butter and jelly, and grilled cheese. We have a few menu items, usually pasta dishes, which are meat free. But these facilities usually go pretty meat heavy because the population has such high protein needs and often have basic "meat and potatoes" food preferences.

When a vegan comes into the facility, we simply cannot accommodate them with what is already in the kitchen. A vegan does not consume any animal products. This includes meat, eggs, dairy, and honey. Sometimes we luck out and find that they are actually vegetarian and someone just mixed up the wording. Another way we can get lucky is if the patient says they're vegan but request meals that are outside of this restriction. Otherwise we have to make a run to the supermarket to buy meals which are more appropriate. Usually the dietary department is not consulted about these admissions before they are in the building. And when they are, it's not like administration is willing to accept an answer they do not want to hear. When I was at Falls View, admissions called me to see if we could take a vegan. The kitchen could barely handle putting out regular meals at the time. I said no. The administrator came storming down to my basement office and was like, "What do you mean we can't accommodate a vegan?! Can't we give them fruit and nuts?!" I had to explain to him that we do not carry nuts in nursing homes and that fruit is not a protein source.

We had a male to female transgendered woman come into the facility. We do not serve transgendered people very often, but it does happen. If it weren't for COVID-19 coming up so often in conversation, you would never know this place was functioning in 2020. Very few people could understand the concept of using her preferred pronouns, which she clearly told Amanda upon admission were "her" and "she." There were a couple of young people who used those pronouns automatically. There were also a few others that you could prompt to use the appropriate wording by modeling it yourself. But the majority could not understand the concept of gender versus sex.

The biggest issue was the roommate situation. It was decided, incorrectly, that she would be placed with a male because she had not had a sex change operation. When Chad returned, he was upset and said that although he lives a very conservative lifestyle, he does not judge those who choose to live differently. I was thinking, "Wow, that's very progressive of him." But then I realized that he was mainly concerned about being sued because transgendered people are a protected class. He reached out to the lawyer to advise him on room placement. She was placed in a private room. When Chad was out one day, this woman was again moved in with a male roommate to make room for a new admission.

One group of people who are not legally protected from discrimination are those with obesity. Another frequent situation I see is facilities accepting bariatric patients when they do not have the proper equipment to care for them. They may have a wheelchair, which accommodates their weight, but body shape also needs to be taken into consideration and is very often overlooked. We picked up a bunch of residents from a facility in another state that had to permanently close due to the pandemic. These people were snapped up like items at a rummage sale. Two of them had wheelchairs which could not fit through most of the doors in the building and for one of them, even that wheelchair was not wide enough. There was no set plan on how we would even be able to get them out in a fire.

Worse than the logistics are the dignity issues around caring for patients when you don't have the proper equipment. We started having more serious discussions about it following a mock survey by corporate. As usual, it did not matter that these women were not receiving the best care until a potential tag was brought up. Social work reached out to Falls View to see if they could accommodate them and they said no. Falls View has been able to handle residents much larger than these women. I had worked with patients over 700 pounds at that site. The building is newer with wider doorways so larger people could move around comfortably anywhere in the building. So, it was obvious that we were still at war with the sister facility.

It was then decided that we would not be transferring these women to a place where they could live in dignity. It may have been due to the fact that our census was dropping again. We had four residents pass away within four days and multiple others discharging from the facility. Instead of letting these women go, Jack took a video of one of them transferring from a Hoyer lift to the wheelchair. He had made an impromptu decision to pull five employees from the therapy department to assist with the demonstration. One of them said, "I don't think you should be filming her." Jack then asked the resident, "You don't mind, do you?" It was obvious that she was uncomfortable by the tone of her voice and her uncertain response of "Umm . . . I guess not." She is a very sweet woman and complied. The staff on her unit adored her and didn't want her to leave but understood that she was not getting the care she needs.

After the ordeal, she had obvious indentations on her legs. Jack brushed it off when the RN running the unit brought this up. The corporate guys are business-men only and do not have legal authority to make clinical judgments, but they do. He then sent this video out via email to multiple others in corporate. One of the ongoing arguments is that the woman recorded was using a thirty-eight-inch wheelchair and required at least a forty-inch wheelchair based on measurements by the therapy director. A chair of this width requires a custom order, which is pricey. As is, the thirty-eight-inch one can't fit through a lot of the tight doorways in the older building. He then approved her for a thirty-six-inch chair.

The therapy director had been working on getting the proper equipment for weeks and kept getting the runaround from corporate. One day after morning report, she started to initiate the conversation with Chad. He said, "Well, isn't it lifestyle factors that got her into this position in the first place?" as if that was even relevant. I decided to stick around and told him that was an overly simplistic understanding of obesity. This woman had been through two unsuccessful bariatric surgeries and had not been asking for extra food during her stay. When he continued making these disrespectful comments, I told him it was not as simple as calories in/calories out. Mitch was chiming in and cackling out loud in agreement with Chad. I told them they were not dietitians. Chad stood up, locked his briefcase, and walked out of the room without saying a word. I was worried that I had pissed him off. But Karen assured me that she knows him well and that his behavior just meant that he realized that the therapy director and I were correct and that he was taking action right away.

When we had no follow-up by the end of the day, I started to worry again that he actually was upset. I felt totally justified in defending these women struggling with weight issues. But maybe I had gone a little too far with the "you're not a dietitian" comment. I reached out to my regional supervisor to give my outsourced company a heads-up in case it ever got back to them. I had mildly annoyed the admin one other time, but never even knew it until it got back to my company. This time felt much more serious. I went home for the weekend worried that there would be some disciplinary action on Monday. But then Monday morning, we were sitting in morning report trying to decide on room changes. They were discussing the possibility of placing three women with obesity in the same quad. Chad joked, "Can the building even structurally support their weight?" I took that as my answer. He was completely unfazed by our conversation the previous week. Even so, I had promised my grandmother I would cool it with calling out the admin on his degrading comments about residents for a while. There was no specific agreed upon amount of time, but three weeks felt reasonable.

After the first day of mock survey, Chad came into my office to speak with Meg. He was all heated about something that had been brought to light and sent out an email about the potential need for administrative cuts. He was in the office discussing the low reimbursement rate for our current patient population. During this conversation, he referred to the residents we cannot profit from as "garbage residents." I was livid. This is a man who will not even swear, but he found it appropriate to literally refer to people as garbage because we couldn't make the big bucks from them.

CHAPTER 15: DOH INSPECTIONS

One day, we were sitting in morning report when someone came into the conference room to tell us that people from the Health Department just walked into the building. Everyone got up and started putting on their masks. At first, I thought we were going to continue the meeting and just pretend that we do so properly masked. And then I realized that we were ending the meeting. All sites owned by this company cancel morning report when someone from the state is in the building. We were encouraged to be on the floor as little as possible in order to avoid scrutiny.

The focus of the inspection was infection control. Once annually, every long-term care facility has a state DOH inspection. The inspectors have a lot of buildings to cover and limited resources so it is usually more than a year between inspections. I believe there is an eighteen-month window in which they need to visit. The annual visits were halted during the pandemic and instead, the focus was on infection control. The state must also investigate all complaints. During the worst of the outbreak, nobody entered the building at all.

During any audit, you spend the majority of the time trying to do your work on the down-low and hoping that nobody summons you for questioning. Corporate also descends upon a building whenever the state is there. I had a bit of a scare because Jack came into my office to ask how my conversation went with the state. Apparently, there had been some discussion about a meal ticket, which I found odd considering this was supposed to be an infection control survey. I spent the rest of the afternoon waiting for them to track me down for questioning. They did not.

The hours went by and staff were getting restless. Another detail about state visits is that you are not allowed to leave the building while they are there. So, when they stay late, it feels a little like a hostage situation. I kept getting up and looking around the building to make sure I wasn't missing the "after party." Every day after the state leaves there is a short meeting among department heads to discuss items which had been a focus of the inspection. Two of the nurses had left. One of them was obviously in trouble. The other was Jill, and her absence did not seem to bother anyone because she had to pick up her child with special needs. Mitch kept trying to draw people's attention to her absence and pointing out the fact that she should not get special treatment. Nobody was in agreement. I found out later that he had a history with Jill when they worked together in another facility. She had called him out for crossing the line with some of the remarks he would make in front of residents.

At one point, there was a group of us in the office biding our time. I was very grateful that Amanda had snacks, because we were starving by seven p.m. One unit manager sat at Meg's desk and munched on a Hostess cake while I destroyed an entire king-sized bag of

M&Ms. I was a little annoyed at having to put in such a long day but felt I had no room to complain since some of the nurses come in at six a.m. The nurse snacking with me was among them and she was also pregnant. Partners at home were getting annoyed trying to plan meals. When were we going to be home? Finally, word got out that the state left the building. It was still a bit disorganized. One of the corporate ladies said we could leave, but Amanda and I did not powerwalk out of the building quickly enough before Chad came around the corner and wanted to hold the meeting.

This meeting took five minutes, tops. The DOH had brought up two issues. The first one had something to do with someone walking with dirty linens held too closely to themselves. The second was that someone went into an area in which they should have been wearing PPE without it on to fetch a glass of water for a resident. We had actually had another infection control survey already. It was a sneak attack on a Saturday. Somehow, we had supposedly passed with flying colors. I don't know how this was possible considering that staffing is never great on weekends.

One of the nurses did get fired for not staying for the duration of the inspection which, to be fair, went until almost eight p.m. She was a newer employee who had not been keeping up well, and this was a convenient excuse. Whenever someone in the building is fired, we need to memorize a new door code. It is generally acknowledged that management staff become scapegoats for poor results during surveys. I have seen two DONs "fired" from the company and then end up in corporate positions within a year. It almost seems like their reward for being willing to take one for the team. I overheard Karen and Mitch gossiping about the DON at a facility they used to work for. One said, "The admin hates her, but they'll keep her around for survey time." A facility must provide a plan of correction showing how they are working to correct deficiencies. A staffing change is quite simple, and much easier than actually fixing the problems.

My outsourced company has a policy that we are all required to sign a document stating that we will contact them immediately when the state enters our facility. We are also not to answer any questions from a surveyor without seeking counsel from them first. We must answer, "Let me check on that and get back to you. Is that okay?" Then we reach out to our company for guidance on exactly what to say and which documentation to provide. At one point, their website even mentioned a guarantee that their dietitians will provide a deficiency-free survey. This claim is no longer there. They must have realized this was a hard guarantee to meet given that they have over a hundred dietitians working in several states. Someone would mess that up sooner or later.

Both of the infectious disease inspections conducted by the DOH since the pandemic have turned up no deficiencies. They may be focused on very specific items at this time. But even prior to the pandemic, these places seemed to get off easily. I don't know how they do it. They must know how to direct the survey-ors' attention where they want it or maybe they're good at negotiating. I was there for the second infectious disease survey and stayed for the meeting afterward, in which there were two situations under scrutiny. I can speculate, but I really don't know how they do it. All I know is that they should not pass these surveys and they do, time and time again. It's obnoxious whenever they do because then they repeatedly cite the deficiency-free surveys as evidence that we did an amazing job handling COVID-19.

As mentioned, there were no in-person surveys during the worst of times. But I feel that the most telling information is in the holes in documentation. I wish they would do a little investigative work into the medical records during this time and in general. Their focus may only be on what they see in person. A simple look into antibiotic stewardship, for example, should turn up some revealing leads. Pam is very stressed about the inappropriate use of antibiotics in the building. One time she said that there were over thirty prescriptions and only three or four meet the criteria for use. The sad thing is that I predict this woman will be the first to be scapegoated when there is a need for one. Her suggestions have been mostly ignored and she has stated how many of the practices in the building go against her ethics. Decisions that she would not be okay with are pushed through when she is not in the building, and this is openly acknowledged during meetings as if this is amusing. Her downfall is already in the works as Karen plants the seeds when Pam isn't present. Right now, they're pretty general—just feeling out who may potentially be on board with throwing her under the bus. Things like, "She's losing her mind." Mitch has been promoted to her right-hand *man*. They will continue to say and do whatever is needed to stay in corporate's good graces. In contrast, Pam's morals slip out from time to time, and this could be her downfall with this company.

CHAPTER 16: NUTRITION IMPLICATIONS

One of the first changes in my practice during this time was initiated by the doctor who was later let go. He asked if I could stop ordering vitamin and mineral supplements. His reasoning was that it would assist in streamlining the medication administration during the pandemic. The supplements I most often recommend are for weight gain or added protein. When I order a vitamin and/or mineral supplement, it is usually due to a confirmed or suspected deficiency. I did not like having this restriction arbitrarily put in place because it meant that I could not provide all of the interventions which could have provided some benefit.

The most drastic change was related to the huge uptick in unintended weight loss in my residents. We receive something called the CASPER (Certification and Survey Provider Enhanced Reports) monthly, which gives statistics on certain quality measures over a specified period of time for the facility with comparisons to the state and national averages. In March, before COVID-19 spread throughout the building, our unintended weight loss average was at 7.1 percent. The state average was 6.4 percent and the national average 5.9 percent. The nursing staff at Dutch Meadows are generally reliable with obtaining these weights—this is not the case in all buildings. When a dietitian is able to catch weight changes early, they can usually work with the team to find a solution before the weight loss becomes significant. So, I was looking forward to finally being in a facility where I could get that figure down below the state average.

The unintended weight loss average jumped almost a full five percentage points in April. Two months after that, it was close to 15 percent. The state average took a while to creep up, even though the city was hit with the virus before us. The state and national averages are currently 9.1 percent and 7.4 percent, respectively. I expect to see the national average continue to climb. New York has had some strong mandates in place for quite some time and should theoretically see improvement. Unfortunately, not all states are taking the crisis seriously and those with a large aging population will struggle.

Oftentimes, I could tell who was affected by the virus by looking at meal intakes alone. I would see a resident who normally cleans their plate have an abrupt and sharp decline in intakes. In the tasks part of the medical record where nursing records data, there would be check boxes in the 76-100 percent column for meal intakes one week and then all of a sudden it would go down to 25-50 percent. Some of these residents did not even seem to realize their own decrease in appetite. I would ask them about it and they would just say the food was not great. The issues with food quality are real. A former food service director at Falls View explained the company's food ordering process. The FSD is instructed to choose the lowest bidder for every food item they need. This not only leads to poor quality food, but there is also no loyalty to any specific vendor, so they do not prioritize the facility. This situation was not new; therefore, it was obvious that the sharp decline in meal intakes was more than a food preference issue.

The kitchen at Dutch Meadows was among the best in the company because the bar was set low. As a clinical dietitian I have few food service responsibilities. I do, however, complete a monthly sanitation audit and I was in awe of Dutch Meadow's kitchen after my time at Falls View because it was clean with no glaring health and safety violations. My last audit at Falls View involved spoiled and undated food, as well as what smelled like an impending electrical fire in the dishwashing area. The food was still cheap; however, the kitchen was run well by a food service director who was willing to put in endless amounts of overtime and even contribute his own money to provide food for special holiday meals for the residents and staff events. The company advertises fresh and local food as well as decorated chefs and skilled dietary staff. In reality, the kitchen is unable to keep skilled staff because they are attracted to higher pay with less stress at gas stations and fast-food restaurants.

This false advertising is pretty common. Another example is that our facility is unable to obtain newspapers for residents who are accustomed to catching up on current events in this way. This amenity is advertised on the website, but the facility stopped paying their bill. Amanda reached out to the company pleading them to pay and was told that they had rush shipped a check that day. The newspaper company never received any payment and cut off the facility from services. According to our current director of operations, when he started his job 2 years ago, there were many vendors who would not service the company. He had to use contacts from prior jobs and he must carefully babysit the company to be sure they are paying the bills.

Many staff also believed that the dwindling meal intakes were related to the lack of activity and feelings of isolation related to this limited means for keeping up with the outside world. This was also true, but again it did not explain such an abrupt change. Residents were depressed about not being able to see their families in person. With group activities halted, they were not even able to socialize as easily with other residents in the building who were going through the same thing. Mealtimes had previously provided some socialization for those who may not be interested in attending group events but were willing to go to the dining room or one of the dayrooms for meals. Lack of activity and isolation definitely contributed to poor appetites, but many also saw food as one of the only things they could look forward to. The illness itself accounted for most of the appetite declines.

There were concerning logistical issues with mealtimes too. With the dining and day rooms closed it would be impossible for all of the residents who needed assistance with feeding or supervision to be properly monitored. While sitting at a table in a dayroom, an aide may be able to feed someone while providing some limited assistance and supervision to others. Most residents were spread out eating in their rooms or just outside of their rooms in the hallway. With understaffing, this was even more of an issue. As mentioned in the preparations chapter, even those staff who took the crash course in providing direct care were not qualified to feed residents. Not only was it likely that residents were not able to eat as much as they could have with assistance, but this was a safety issue as well. The aides provide pacing reminders and a second set of eyes to ensure that everyone gets food items with the proper textures/consistencies. Aspiration and choking were a real concern.

During the worst of the outbreak, dietary aides were no longer allowed to enter the units. The meal trays were placed on the carts and dropped off at the closed double doors for the nursing aides to pick up and bring onto the unit to distribute. The cart pass off was not a smooth transition at first. There was a lack of communication; sometimes the food would be outside of the unit getting cold with nobody realizing that it had been delivered. Getting the trays, plates, bowls, and utensils returned was equally tricky. This created a lot of tension between dietary and nursing. Some facilities used single use items during this time to minimize staff exposure to contaminated dishware, but I don't think we did this at any point.

Amanda and her activities aides were always coming up with creative ideas to boost morale. They used to have a little store where residents could come and buy snacks and socialize. Since the residents could no longer leave their units, they came up with snack cart ideas. One of the most popular was walking tacos. These are tacos that are made in chip bags. There was a day of mocktails; the snack cart looked like a fancy traveling bar that day. Sometimes there were healthier snack options, but usually they were fun, energy-dense foods. I appreciated that Amanda would ask me who was struggling with weight loss so they could pay particular attention to these residents.

Hospitals in New York City started having critical shortages of tube feed pumps because there were so many people on ventilators who required tube feeding. Pumps are only required for patients who need to have the formula infused over several hours per day. Ideally, you want to mimic a regular eating schedule as much as possible, so for patients who are able, you can use a syringe to feed cans of formula around mealtimes. This is called bolus feeding. Others, such as those who are at risk for aspiration or who are being fed directly into the small intestine, require a more gradual feeding.

Soon the pump shortage affected the entire country. I had two residents who were on pumps which could give automatic water flushes at the same time as the tube feed rather than requiring someone to administer the flushes by hand. I much prefer this method because it minimizes the risk for human error. And with staffing shortages, I did not want that risk. But the good pumps disappeared with no explanation. I assume that the company found some way to make a little money by switching these in-demand pumps out for cheaper ones. I was able to advance one of the residents to bolus feedings. The other has a very involved wife who would not hesitate to hold staff accountable if she noted signs of dehydration during one of her daily video chats.

The SLP was seeing many of our residents return from the hospital with swallowing deficits. There were residents who enjoyed regular meals before who had to start receiving a mechanically altered diet. The most restrictive is the pureed diet, which is not appetizing and increases the risk for protein-calorie malnutrition due to poor acceptance and the fact that these meals have to be watered down to some extent to create the right texture. Some also require thickened liquids because regular fluids can slip down into someone's windpipe if their swallowing function is not well coordinated. Our SLP became so busy with all of our COVID-19 related swallowing deficits that she described her daily interactions as feeling kind of like speed dating. She was running around trying to collect the most useful information from as many people as she could in the shortest period of time. There was so much added work that a second full-time SLP was recently added to the team.

Chapter 17: No Learning from Past Mistakes

By mid-July, we had been accepting new admissions for over a month. Things were starting to feel back to normal. I had taken a week of vacation time at the end of June and came back to a full workload with all of the new residents. Chad announced on Monday, July 20th that we were now at 93 percent capacity and he had received a complimentary email from corporate about it. Not long beforehand, the administrators in the company had received a not-so-friendly email about the need to prioritize the census above all else.

It became impossible to ignore the fact that we still had active COVID-19 infections in the building, but we had gone right back to the denial phase we were in back in April when we allowed the illness to spread unchecked. The only difference was that now the residents were kept on their own units. The staff had become a little too comfortable with this situation. The DON brought up that staff were becoming unprofessional and swearing openly, for example, because there were no residents out of their units. The public spaces in the building have become more like the staff home while the resident home has shrunk down to the narrow hallways of the units.

All through June we had people going to the hospital and testing positive. Almost everyone we sent out to the hospital tested positive. The admissions director confirmed several people who had gone out since the facility's reopening and tested positive. Some of them were people who had previously tested positive. Others were new cases in residents in the building who had managed to not get the illness during the main outbreak (62, 65). There were also new admissions who either came in from the hospital with the illness or picked it up in our facility (63, 64).

Falls View sent multiple requests to take back one of their residents. The only catch was that they requested a negative test result before bringing him back. This was customary at most healthcare facilities by this point. Dutch Meadows, however, did not want to risk having a positive test in the facility, which could require restarting the twenty-eight-day period during which we could not take new admissions. One day, I received a phone call from a dietitian at one of the hospitals which was taking care of two of our residents who had tested positive. As far as Dutch Meadows was concerned, if the positive test did not occur in the building, we were in the clear. Chad tried to justify this once by stating that our residents could be contracting the illness in the hospitals while waiting to be seen in the emergency rooms.

Care conferences for the rehabilitation unit became beyond frustrating. A woman came to her conference with obvious cold symptoms. She was losing her voice and had a cough. A chest X-ray had been ordered with the results negative for pneumonia. She brought up her concern about COVID-19 infection because she did not want to return to her family and get people sick. Sue began telling her that she did not have COVID-19 based on her X-ray result since she had heard these types of explanations from the nursing department. Although all departments are required to attend the care conferences, nursing rarely makes an appearance or attempts to follow up for the resident meetings on this unit. I cut in at this point and "clarified" that the only way to be certain that she did not have the virus would be to have COVID-19 testing. The chest X-ray usually turned up nothing in our COVID-19 positive residents. I did not go on to tell her that the facility would be unwilling to test her because they didn't want her to ruin their ability to bring in more people to make money. One of the therapists and I encouraged her to advocate for herself and bring it up with the NP.

At this time, the facility had not received the test results from the staff from the week beforehand. I wondered if a similar lab issue was contributing to the facility's hesitance to test residents. I asked Mitch for his opinion on the issue. I said that I found it sketchy that we weren't at least testing the residents with symptoms who were being followed on the COVID line lists. He said that it was because none of these people had symptoms that could not be explained by other medical issues. We had cycled back to explaining away symptoms rather than testing for the illness. Since we had several people who tested positive in the hospital and others in-house spiking fevers and developing other symptoms, we should have been testing.

At another care conference on this day, the friend of one of the residents with a quickly approaching discharge date asked if she could get documentation for a negative COVID test before the resident's return to the senior community where she lived. This was required. The facility was looking into whether or not we could use the negative test that we required from the hospital rather than provide a test result at the end of her stay. I interpreted the facility's efforts at avoiding testing at all costs as acknowledgement of the strong possibility that COVID-19 was still present in the building. At this point, Falls View was testing everyone prior to discharge. From mid-June through early August, we had been in a cycle of residents going out to the hospital over the weekend and testing positive in the hospital.

This prompted more conversation around the facility's favorite conspiracy theory that the hospital was purposely coming up with positive results in order to get more reimbursement. Pam said that the hospital earned an additional four hundred dollars per day for each COVID-19 positive resident. Karen decided to explore this theory further. During morning report, she had everyone help her make a list of all the residents we'd had who tested positive over the past several weeks. Then we looked up which hospitals admitted them. At first she thought she was really onto something as the same hospital had admitted the first several positives. Then she realized there were at least two separate hospitals testing all of our patients positive. This research activity did not support the theory unless we wanted to get really bold and accuse all of the hospitals of participating in this conspiracy.

Let's take a moment to briefly visit the profile of the typical DON. Ours very much fit the characteristics I'd experienced in DONs at other facilities. They are usually middle-aged female smokers. They generally seem to enjoy the attention they receive in morning report and interject gossip and personal stories into the meeting. They often wear dresses—this may be their way to celebrate the fact that they have climbed out of the role of having to work the floor. Most annoyingly, they surround themselves with their crew. When they start at a new facility, they will bring an entourage from their previous job. Karen met all of these criteria and had brought on Pam and Mitch. These three hold the highest clinical positions in the building. The doctors technically have the most clinical authority; however, it is these three who attend all of the meetings and ingratiate themselves regularly with the administrator and corporate office.

One of our recent COVID-19 cases prompted Chad to say that technically all of the staff on that unit should be furloughed and we should be returning to full PPE. This was not happening. After a positive result came back the previous week, we were supposed to take it upon ourselves to let the facility know if we had been exposed to that resident. This would result in a two-week unpaid furlough because any staff who had not been using the correct PPE were breaking the rules, even though PPE was not being provided. We were also told that this would not be an issue because we were doing the right thing. It was implied that coming forward would likely have resulted in some type of disciplinary action for not taking the proper precautions.

There had been no gowns available outside of the units for weeks. I believe that the rehab unit still had the communal gowns available hanging inside the rooms for each of the dialysis residents and new admissions. N95 respirators had not been allowed since June 19th. The masks at the staff entrance into the building had not been stocked for months. The hand sanitizer dispenser on the wall had not been maintained and was a disgusting mess of insects stuck on the old drying product. Even the masks at the main entrance were no longer consistently available.

I had vented about this situation in front of Mitch. He said these stations couldn't be stocked because people would grab handfuls of masks and hoard them. It would be impossible to keep these items stocked. This was interesting because they had been adequately stocked for a while and we did not have a shortage of these items. In fact, there was a new mandate that facilities needed to have at least a sixty-day's supply of PPE. I mentally compared this to the toilet paper shortage we experienced for weeks when the pandemic first hit. If people believe they will have reliable access to these items, they will not hoard them.

Then I learned why Mitch was parroting corporate's weak explanations behind not testing the symptomatic residents or providing PPE. He seemed a little too competent to actually believe any of it. When he mentioned that he was hired with the promise of an eventual implied promotion to a corporate position, it all made sense. He did not want to mess this up by publicly disagreeing with their flawed reasoning. So, he wasn't stupid—just a complete sellout.

While Pam was out for two weeks, PPE was put back in use on the rehab unit. Of course, it was due to pressure from the outside. And of course, the staff were blamed. Chad said the staff were supposed to be wearing PPE, but they hadn't been complying and it was time to accept this as the new norm. It's impossible to comply with wearing PPE when it's not provided. Before Pam had left, she listed off the PPE requirements of a gown, masks, and goggles. Goggles?! This had literally never been in use before and now it was casually being listed as if we had been using them all along.

Pam was not thrilled with the new PPE rules put in place while she was away. Learning them was kind of like memorizing the rules of a board game. You wear a gown and face shield on the unit at all times. Simple. There are four colors outside of resident rooms. Residents in the yellow rooms are on their two-week new admission precautions. Residents in the red rooms have a known exposure. Residents in the white rooms have completed their two-week precautionary period and will soon be moved off the unit. Residents in pink rooms are COVID-19 positive. You can keep on the same gown for the same color rooms only. For this reason, they tried to room residents together who had been admitted around the same time because the precaution status was based on the person who had been there for the shortest period of time.

I was excited about the new face shields for about five minutes. They looked cool but fogged up very quickly. One of the therapy staff showed me a sticker over the front which is tricky to find but improves the visibility a bit once it's peeled off. Therapy has always been the most reliable department when it comes to PPE use. I brought in safety goggles because they fogged up less. Even the new PPE protocol wasn't followed through on for very long. After about a week, the face shields were not stocked. Weeks afterward, I was gowning up to attend a care conference on the rehab unit when Pam dropped off some face shields because corporate was in the building that day.

While the facility had chosen to ignore some of the mandates putting restrictions in place, it also chose to maintain some of the restrictions which had been lifted. The reasoning behind both were for convenience only, not for well-being of the residents or staff. Sue was manager on duty one weekend and brought up the fact that the residents were always in bed and getting depressed. The staff were overstretched, particularly on weekends, and were not able to interact much with their residents. Karen told Sue to stop talking about it because she didn't want to hear "Debbie Downer" stuff that day.

The mandate banning visitors had been lifted a month prior. There were certain guidelines that we needed to follow to allow visitors back. First, only 10 percent of the residents could have visitors on any given day. Only two visitors were allowed at a time per resident and at least one of them needed to be older than eighteen years of age. Everyone needed to have their temperature taken, be masked, and follow all of the social distancing guidelines. A plan had to be submitted to the DOH detailing how we would be implementing these visitation guidelines.

Right before limited visitation was allowed again, we discussed what needed to be done to make this happen. We would need to give visitors a simple handout detailing the rules. We also talked about the possibility of setting up a big awning outside so that there would be more space for those waiting to visit a loved one. Although we could have visitors as of July 10th, we were told it would most likely be at least August 1st before we could accommodate them. At the start of September, there had been no updates on the status of the visitation plan. Pam said that we would not be allowing visitors back because it would put our residents at unnecessary risk. The only reason for not allowing visitors was laziness and not wanting any scrutiny by family members. The facility could put literally any demands in place to allow for visitors as long as it was detailed in the plan submitted to the DOH. We could theoretically require COVID-19 testing for visitors. The original idea proposed in July about having outdoor visits would have been great, but now it had been put off for so long that we were entering fall. I believe this stalling was on purpose.

There are plenty of other, less serious examples of the facility using the pandemic to their benefit. The admissions director had worked in the building for over two decades and brought up to Jack that the place was worse than she had ever seen it. He said it was due to COVID-19. She is bold and brought up that many of these cut corners were not due to the pandemic, but only to save money. There is no longer an employee of the month or star designations for staff who have been doing an exemplary job. The landscaping hadn't been tended to all summer. There were no flowers, the weeds were out of control, and some potted trees had never been put in the ground. They sat outside the social work office, slowly dying behind some shrubbery. Jack told the admissions director that he didn't have time for this and walked away. Sometimes corporate doesn't even have the decency to put in the effort to pretend to care.

While limiting resident exposure to illness was used as an excuse to keep families out, staff were showing up sick to work. Dealing with the pandemic should have increased awareness of disease spread with overall improved sick etiquette. When we were finally free from COVID-19 for at least a couple of weeks, the weather started to change, and with it came the expected colds. Karen was out sick for a couple of days. When she returned, she was still very sick and complained that she should not be there.

Then Sue fell ill but continued to show up at work. On a Thursday, she was coughing and gagging so badly it was causing a scene. Karen said that she thought Sue caught what she had. While Sue was out of the room, I said that it was inappropriate for people to show up to work so sick. Nobody responded. Neither Karen nor Sue took it upon themselves to wear a mask, yet they insisted on sitting at the conference table during their illnesses. The illness spread to the admission director and all of the unit managers.

Nobody has a role which is so important that the place would grind to a halt without them. Even though we were being tested weekly for COVID-19, that didn't mean that colds and other illnesses weren't still disruptive for staff. These illnesses could be life-threatening for a resident. We had not learned basic consideration for others.

The place likes to pick and choose which of "Crazy Cuomo's" statements to be in agreement with and during which times. They like the one about it being now known that the majority of COVID-19 cases were introduced into facilities by asymptomatic visitors and staff unknowingly bringing it in. Previously, the facility was blaming Cuomo for introducing the illness by requiring nursing homes to accept COVID-19 positive residents from the hospital. Now that we don't want to deal with the inconvenience of setting up visitation, we're cool with letting it go. In reality, neither of these scenarios brought the illness into our facility. We have a very vulnerable population. People need to go out for dialysis and chemotherapy treatments. Sooner or later, one of these residents or a new admission is going to unknowingly bring it back.

Chapter 18: Will These Places Ever Be Held Accountable?

Five months after our first diagnosed COVID-19 cases in the building, we still have cases pop up occasionally. At this point, we have sixty-five recognized cases tied to our building. And by recognized, I mean from my own list of residents who tested positive, which I put together from multiple sources. This is the list I use when putting together COVID-19 related weight loss audits required by my outsourced company. This is the only way to ensure accuracy because many of our confirmed positive cases do not have it listed in their diagnoses list. The current death toll from the illness is nineteen residents. This means almost 30 percent of our residents who tested positive passed away. This figure is high even in this population. I always wondered if the facility ever considered that it might look worse to have a higher percentage of deaths from the illness than the percentage of total residents contracting the illness. The former suggests that not all of the cases were reported.

This includes cases from both the facility and the hospital. There was a time when facilities were taking advantage of a loophole that counted deaths at hospitals separately from those at nursing homes to avoid double counting. If they sent a struggling resident to the hospital to die, they didn't have to count the death in their own figures. I never learned the fate of all of our residents who went out to the hospital and did not return. The deaths may be higher as many of our COVID-19 positive deaths occurred well after the acute illness. In the facility, residents who never returned to baseline following the illness continue to die off slowly. All of our dialysis residents contracted the illness. Everyone who was allowed to spend time in the dining room after Pam had closed it down got the virus. Most of them are dead now. I don't know the figures actually reported because this information is not readily shared even with the group in morning report. I would guess that it is a lot lower.

But the actual figure is so much higher than mine. The facility only tested people when the DOH was breathing down its neck. And the DOH has a lot to deal with during a pandemic. They don't have the resources to be full-time babysitters. I have another list of at least a dozen other residents who are probable cases. Most of these residents have passed. Some of them were the roommates of known positives. My list of probable cases is only a fraction of those uncaught cases. I am not privy to certain information such as line lists. These are only the symptomatic residents who stood out to me for one reason or another.

I would guess that most residents and staff were exposed. People out in the public are required to quarantine for two weeks if they travel to an area with a high risk of transmission. We were all in a building for a long period of time in which there were obvious cases and were expected to believe contradictory information. At times we were told that there weren't enough tests. I never fully believed this. Even if that were the case, what excuse is there for not isolating even the very symptomatic residents?

The leadership in the building is baffled and annoyed anytime they are called out on anything. During a mock survey there were some suggestions for improvement. Most notably, they pointed out that it is unacceptable to not stock PPE at the staff entrance. They caught staff walking unmasked through the building upon arrival to get masks in the front, which is the only place where they are somewhat reliably stocked. They had refused to stock the staff entrance long ago because they suspected staff were taking some home to their families.

As usual, we only look into solutions when forced from the outside. Jack suggested we have staff walk from the staff parking lot in the back around the building to the front entrance. Karen pointed out that this is not sustainable because it is a long walk riddled with potholes and poses a potential lawsuit in the winter. There are simple solutions which do not put the inconvenience or blame on staff. The easiest option would be to give everyone his or her allotment of PPE at the beginning of the week. And why not throw in a few extra surgical masks for them to bring home to their families? It would be a small gesture of appreciation considering these "heroes" were forced to put their own health and the health of their families at risk and didn't see a dime in hazard pay.

The chosen solution was to have a nurse stand at the staff entrance to take temperatures and give out masks to the staff arriving for the 7 a.m. to 3 p.m. shift. There was no coverage for the two other shifts. Meg was chosen for this task since she arrives so early in the morning. For the first several weeks she was forced to search the building like on a scavenger hunt trying to track down PPE. When she asked the staff privileged enough to have access to the PPE, she was told that there was none available. She had to be resourceful and demanding to obtain the masks and thermometer needed to perform the task to which she was assigned.

There was a mandatory webinar some staff were required to attend about COVID-19 preparedness. Karen said, "Why do we have to attend? We basically wrote the guide on COVID-19 response. Are we the ones presenting?" This type of delusional thinking continues despite the fact that we have had so many cases and deaths. Chad keeps repeating that we will probably have to continue the mandatory staff testing at least until November because the rules regarding continued testing will be dependent on the election. Chad believes if Trump wins, this will go on forever. If Biden wins, COVID-19 will disappear. A COVID-19 denier has no place in healthcare. The administrator's role at these facilities needs some adjusting. Most do not have the educational background to be given autonomy to make clinical decisions which can have huge health and safety implications for residents and staff. The upper-level clinical staff are so focused on pleasing the administrator in order to keep their jobs, they do not *do* their jobs. Pleasing the administrator is simple if you're willing to preach messages against science or government regulation.

This has come easily to Karen. A recent example that I found shocking even in our facility came about when Pam brought up the flu vaccines which will soon be available to staff. More staff are resistant to getting them this year because everyone wears a mask due to COVID-19. In previous years, staff who were on the fence about getting the vaccine could be swayed by the fact that they would be required to wear a mask at all times in the building once it was officially deemed flu season. This combined with the anti-vaxxer movement gaining momentum as the country struggles through the pandemic has led to the risk of fewer staff receiving the vaccine. Pam said that if at least 90 percent of staff in the building does not receive the vaccine, the facility will be fined.

Karen responded, "We are being forced to put mercury into our bodies." I find it very disturbing that our director of nursing was spouting anti-vaxxer propaganda. Thimerosal is a compound which contains trace amounts of mercury, which is used as a preservative in some flu vaccines in multi-dose vials. This was to keep the vaccine from becoming contaminated as each individual needle was put into the vial. Now most flu vaccines are put into single-dose vials, so no preservative is needed. However, there were no reputable scientific studies which found a link between thimerosal and autism or any other conditions. Yet she is willing to spread this misinformation rather than do her research as a healthcare professional.

Chad is an excellent orator and occasionally gives pep talks that are heartfelt and motivational. We sometimes joke that we hate when he comes in on time because morning report takes longer, but I do enjoy the speeches. The most recent one was very bleak, but he is skillful enough to make us feel appreciated and valuable. The Centers for Medicare and Medicaid Services (CMS) is working on setting new minimum staffing levels. I don't believe there has ever been an official required staffing ratio in New York. So, the pandemic may have brought to light the need for one. While CMS is coming up with these required staffing levels, the facilities have the responsibility of officially setting their own in the meantime. And this level will be low because we must be able to show that we're able to meet these self-declared minimum staffing levels or else we have to discharge residents to the hospital or elsewhere to receive the proper care. Eventually there will also be a hotline. There were no details on the hotline—my impression is that it will be a pool of floating staff that the state is putting together.

Also, there are fewer school programs now available for people entering the field, and those programs that still exist are not offered as frequently. This is tough work and it is very scary to consider that we may not have enough staff to make up for the ones who burn out and need to leave, even temporarily. And with less staff, employees will burn out at a more rapid rate. Unfortunately, the White House administration also required the CDC to update their policy on testing for COVID-19 to state that testing asymptomatic people is unnecessary. This was reversed quickly, but it added fuel to the administrator's belief that all government-imposed guidelines are completely arbitrary and there is no scientific basis behind them. And who can blame him? When you don't have a science background and you see that politicians are not always following the advice of experts, there is no way to know what to believe. This is still very much an unfolding situation that will most likely, unfortunately, get much worse before it gets better.

There was recent news that post-mortem COVID-19 testing may be required for suspected cases. The staff at Dutch Meadows are not happy about it, but I think it could save many lives. The facility got away with many probable COVID-19 cases by not testing sick residents. If the resident was a DNR, they could pass away and the facility would not have to count the case. This requirement may force more facilities to test their sick residents while they are still alive since they can't get away with it anymore if they die. It could also save the lives of many around them, because those cases which were previously ignored would be forced out into the open, which would require separating them from other residents. Removing the motivation for unethical staff to coerce patients into accepting DNR/DNH status could also save lives.

I hope we continue to see more legislation passed that will hold these private companies accountable. This will not happen until all loopholes are exposed. It would be better for some of these companies to go under than to reward them for bad behavior. Unfortunately, the responsible companies may suffer the most. My friend working at one of the nicer nursing homes said the company is millions of dollars in debt from this year alone. This facility has been mentioned a couple of times throughout this story during examples of responsible practices. The company had initiated widespread staff and resident testing and provided adequate PPE. They paid staff hazard pay. They have only one facility so there was no option to shuffle residents around within the company to assist in minimizing losses during admission freezes. If these companies are allowed to continue having full autonomy, the good ones will most likely be absorbed by the ones willing to cut corners.

The pandemic has brought many issues to the forefront, but these are not new issues and they are not uncommon. Until changes are made, the most vulnerable people will continue to be exploited by the industry. But the situation is not completely without hope. People are speaking out and it's having a positive impact. In September, a federal agency required nursing homes to facilitate in-person visitation. Nursing homes can now face sanctions for blanket bans on visitation. My workplace was miraculously able to safely accommodate this once it became required. Without pushback from people who care, these residents would have been restricted to seeing their family indefinitely through the glass.